Great English Short Stories

Roald Dahl · Katherine Mansfield
Alun Lewis · James Joyce
Alan Sillitoe · John Wain

*Edited by Horst Bodden,
Herbert Kaußen and Rudi Renné*

Ernst Klett Schulbuchverlag
Stuttgart Düsseldorf Berlin Leipzig

Acknowledgments

R. Dahl, *Dip in the Pool* from *Someone Like You* (Michael Joseph, London, 1961) is printed by permission of Mohrbooks, Zurich.

K. Mansfield, *The Doll's House* is taken from the collection *The Dove's Nest*, 1923.

A. Lewis, *The Lapse* from *The Last Inspection* is reprinted by permission of George Allen & Unwin Ltd., London.

J. Joyce, *Eveline* from *Dubliners* is reprinted by permission of The Society of Authors as the literary representative of the Estate of James Joyce.

A. Sillitoe, *On Saturday Afternoon* from *The Loneliness of the Long-Distance Runner* is reprinted by permission of the author. Copyright © Alan Sillitoe, 1959.

J. Wain, *A Message from the Pig-Man* from *Nuncle and Other Stories* (Macmillan Publishers Ltd., London, 1960) is reprinted by permission of the author.

The stories by Katherine Mansfield, Alun Lewis, James Joyce and John Wain are also available on cassette (Klettnummer 57867).

Gedruckt auf Papier aus chlorfrei gebleichtem Zellstoff, säurefrei.

1. Auflage   1 21 20 19 18 | 1998 97 96 95

Alle Drucke dieser Auflage können im Unterricht nebeneinander benutzt werden; sie sind untereinander unverändert. Die letzte Zahl bezeichnet das Jahr dieses Druckes.
© dieser Ausgabe Ernst Klett Schulbuchverlag GmbH, Stuttgart 1979.
Alle Rechte vorbehalten.
Umschlagfoto: Robert Maier, Anthony-Verlag, Starnberg.
Druck: Wilhelm Röck, Weinsberg. Printed in Germany.
ISBN 3-12-578600-2

Contents

Introduction	4
Roald Dahl Dip in the Pool (1953)*	6
Katherine Mansfield The Doll's House (1923)	16
Alun Lewis The Lapse (1942)	23
James Joyce Eveline (1914)	26
Alan Sillitoe On Saturday Afternoon (1959)	30
John Wain A Message from the Pig-Man (1960)	37
Study Material:	
Roald Dahl Dip in the Pool	44
Katherine Mansfield The Doll's House	49
Alun Lewis The Lapse	55
James Joyce Eveline	59
Alan Sillitoe On Saturday Afternoon	63
John Wain A Message from the Pig-Man	69
Glossary of Literary Terms	74

*The figures in brackets give the year of the first publication in book form.

Introduction

The title and general character of this collection of short stories need some explanation. Each of the six stories may be qualified as "English", because the language used in them is "British English". In addition, they are all notable examples of the modern short story, representing outstanding literary quality as well as modernity of theme and form. It was especially James Joyce and Katherine Mansfield who greatly contributed to the creation of the modern English short story, whose authors no longer attempt to make daily life more entertaining by inventing exotic plots. Instead, modern story writers have tended to base their narratives on their own experience; here the focus is much more on the less spectacular aspects of life, on the significance underlying what is apparently trivial. The result of such perceptive writing is perfection of form, harmony of theme and structure, and precision of style to reveal the subtleties of the human mind and of human behaviour.

In selecting the fiction for this course, not only the literary merit and modernity of the stories were considered, but also the didactic purposes of a course in reading fiction. For example, besides established classics (Joyce and Mansfield) and highly esteemed contemporaries (Wain and Sillitoe), Alun Lewis and Roald Dahl also provide both good writing and an illustration of narrative technique. The themes of these six stories seek to appeal to and motivate the adolescent student, who himself is increasingly confronted with the complexities of human life. In this phase of his life he is making far-reaching decisions about his own life, which is made up of successes and failures, of opportunities and frustrations. These stories convey the fact that life is a continual challenge to the individual, through childhood, youth, and adulthood; life is a delicate balance of imprisonment and the opportunities of escape from it. In *A Message from the Pig-Man* six-year-old Ekky is confused by the intricacies of adult behaviour and is too young to understand it. The Burnell children, in *The Doll's House*, have reached the point where they may question their family's prejudices of social status and respectability, with Kezia even ignoring the social barriers. Sillitoe's boy-narrator has experienced and understood the hopelessness of depression and suicide and states his will to stay alive. Joyce's Eveline is thrown into the inner conflict of choosing between her family and a new life in a far-away country. *The Lapse* by Alun Lewis is about the vain attempt to escape from everyday routine, which, however, also provides comfort. And Dahl, in his humorous and ironic treatment of this theme of imprisonment and escape demonstrates the unforeseeable complications when the protagonist of the story tries to push his luck too far.

The *Study Material* in this collection is of particular importance for a successful course on reading short fiction. The systematic increase of the students' linguistic competence and the rational acquisition of the methods of text analysis need to be carefully graded and linguistically based. Therefore this *Study Material* offers a variety of guidance to help the student prepare for the complex stage of text interpretation.

The *biographical notes* provide concise information about the literary "background", the *vocabulary lists* are to make the reading of the texts as entertaining and timesaving as possible. Moreover, additional *linguistic exercises* (revision or further practice) and *comprehension questions* are all intended to ensure comprehension and increase word power. Finally, the *Glossary of Literary Terms* should be a continual source of reliable information in the field of correct terminology when working on or discussing the structures and themes of these stories.

Roald Dahl

Dip in the Pool

On the morning of the third day, the sea calmed. Even the most delicate passengers – those who had not been seen around the ship since sailing time – emerged from their cabins and crept on to the sun deck where the deck steward gave them chairs and tucked rugs around their legs and left them lying in rows,
5 their faces up turned to the pale, almost heatless January sun.

It had been moderately rough the first two days, and this sudden calm and the sense of comfort that it brought created a more genial atmosphere over the whole ship. By the time evening came, the passengers, with twelve hours of good weather behind them, were beginning to feel confident, and at eight
10 o'clock that night the main dining-room was filled with people eating and drinking with the assured, complacent air of seasoned sailors.

The meal was not half over when the passengers became aware, by the slight friction between their bodies and the seats of their chairs, that the big ship had actually started rolling again. It was very gentle at first, just a slow, lazy leaning
15 to one side, then to the other, but it was enough to cause a subtle, immediate change of mood over the whole room. A few of the passengers glanced up from their food, hesitating, waiting, almost listening for the next roll, smiling nervously, little secret glimmers of apprehension in their eyes. Some were completely unruffled, some were openly smug, a number of the smug ones making
20 jokes about food and weather in order to torture the few who were beginning to suffer. The movement of the ship then became rapidly more and more violent, and only five or six minutes after the first roll had been noticed, she was swinging heavily from side to side, the passengers bracing themselves in their chairs, leaning against the pull as in a car cornering.

25 At last the really bad roll came, and Mr William Botibol, sitting at the purser's table, saw his plate of poached turbot with hollandaise sauce sliding suddenly away from under his fork. There was a flutter of excitement, everybody reaching for plates and wineglasses. Mrs Renshaw, seated at the purser's right, gave a little scream and clutched that gentleman's arm.

30 "Going to be a dirty night," the purser said, looking at Mrs Renshaw. "I think it's blowing up for a very dirty night." There was just the faintest sugges-

tion of relish in the way he said it.

A steward came hurrying up and sprinkled water on the tablecloth between the plates. The excitement subsided. Most of the passengers continued with their meal. A small number, including Mrs Renshaw, got carefully to their feet and threaded their ways with a kind of concealed haste between the tables and through the doorway.

"Well," the purser said, "there she goes." He glanced around with approval at the remainder of his flock who were sitting quiet, looking complacent, their faces reflecting openly that extraordinary pride that travellers seem to take in being recognized as "good sailors".

When the eating was finished and the coffee had been served, Mr Botibol, who had been unusually grave and thoughtful since the rolling started, suddenly stood up and carried his cup of coffee around to Mrs Renshaw's vacant place, next to the purser. He seated himself in her chair, then immediately leaned over and began to whisper urgently in the purser's ear. "Excuse me," he said, "but could you tell me something, please?"

The purser, small and fat and red, bent forward to listen. "What's the trouble, Mr Botibol?"

"What I want to know is this." The man's face was anxious and the purser was watching it. "What I want to know is will the captain already have made his estimate on the day's run – you know, for the auction pool? I mean before it began to get rough like this?"

The purser, who had prepared himself to receive a personal confidence, smiled and leaned back in his seat to relax his full belly. "I should say so – yes," he answered. He didn't bother to whisper his reply, although automatically he lowered his voice, as one does when answering a whisperer.

"About how long ago do you think he did it?"

"Some time this afternoon. He usually does it in the afternoon."

"About what time?"

"Oh, I don't know. Around four o'clock I should guess."

"Now tell me another thing. How does the captain decide which number it shall be? Does he take a lot of trouble over that?"

The purser looked at the anxious frowning face of Mr Botibol and he smiled, knowing quite well what the man was driving at. "Well, you see, the captain has a little conference with the navigating officer, and they study the weather and a lot of other things, and then they make their estimate."

Mr Botibol nodded, pondering this answer for a moment. Then he said, "Do you think the captain knew there was bad weather coming today?"

"I couldn't tell you," the purser replied. He was looking into the small black eyes of the other man, seeing the two single little sparks of excitement dancing in their centres. "I really couldn't tell you, Mr Botibol. I wouldn't know."

"If this gets any worse it might be worth buying some of the low numbers. What do you think?" The whispering was more urgent, more anxious now.

"Perhaps it will," the purser said. "I doubt whether the old man allowed for a really rough night. It was pretty calm this afternoon when he made his estimate."

The others at the table had become silent and were trying to hear, watching the purser with that intent, half-cocked, listening look that you can see also at the race track when they are trying to overhear a trainer talking about his chance: the slightly open lips, the upstretched eyebrows, the head forward and cocked a little to one side – that desperately straining, half-hypnotized, listening look that comes to all of them when they are hearing something straight from the horse's mouth.

"Now suppose *you* were allowed to buy a number, which one would *you* choose today?" Mr Botibol whispered.

"I don't know what the range is yet," the purser patiently answered. "They don't announce the range till the auction starts after dinner. And I'm really not very good at it anyway. I'm only the purser, you know."

At that point Mr Botibol stood up. "Excuse me, all," he said, and he walked carefully away over the swaying floor between the other tables, and twice he had to catch hold of the back of a chair to steady himself against the ship's roll.

"The sun deck, please," he said to the elevator man.

The wind caught him full in the face as he stepped out on to the open deck. He staggered and grabbed hold of the rail and held on tight with both hands, and he stood there looking out over the darkening sea where the great waves were welling up high and white horses were riding against the wind with plumes of spray behind them as they went.

"Pretty bad out there, wasn't it, sir?" the elevator man said on the way down.

Mr Botibol was combing his hair back into place with a small red comb. "Do you think we've slackened speed at all on account of the weather?" he asked.

"Oh my word yes, sir. We slackened off considerable since this started. You got to slacken off speed in weather like this or you'll be throwing the passengers all over the ship."

Down in the smoking-room people were already gathering for the auction. They were grouping themselves politely around the various tables, the men a little stiff in their dinner jackets, a little pink and overshaved and stiff beside their cool white-armed women. Mr Botibol took a chair close to the auctioneer's table. He crossed his legs, folded his arms, and settled himself in his seat with the rather desperate air of a man who has made a tremendous decision and refuses to be frightened.

The pool, he was telling himself, would probably be around seven thousand dollars. That was almost exactly what it had been the last two days with the numbers selling for between three and four hundred apiece. Being a British ship they did it in pounds, but he liked to do his thinking in his own currency. Seven thousand dollars was plenty of money. My goodness, yes! And what he would do he would get them to pay him in hundred-dollar bills and he would take it ashore in the inside pocket of his jacket. No problem there. And right away, yes right away, he would buy a Lincoln convertible. He would pick it up on the way from the ship and drive it home just for the pleasure of seeing Ethel's face when she came out the front door and looked at it. Wouldn't that be something, to see Ethel's face when he glided up to the door in a brand-new pale-green Lincoln convertible! Hello, Ethel, honey, he would say, speaking very casual. I just thought I'd get you a little present. I saw it in the window as I went by, so I thought of you and how you were always wanting one. You like it, honey? he would say. You like the colour? And then he would watch her face.

The auctioneer was standing up behind his table now. "Ladies and gentlemen!" he shouted. "The captain has estimated the day's run, ending midday tomorrow, at five hundred and fifteen miles. As usual we will take the ten numbers on either side of it to make up the range. That makes it five hundred and five to five hundred and twenty-five. And of course for those who think the true figure will be still farther away, there'll be 'low field' and 'high field' sold separately as well. Now, we'll draw the first numbers out of the hat . . . here we are . . . five hundred and twelve?"

The room became quiet. The people sat still in their chairs, all eyes watching the auctioneer. There was a certain tension in the air, and as the bids got higher, the tension grew. This wasn't a game or a joke; you could be sure of that by the way one man would look across at another who had raised his bid – smiling perhaps, but only the lips smiling, the eyes bright and absolutely cold.

Number five hundred and twelve was knocked down for one hundred and ten pounds. The next three or four numbers fetched roughly the same amount.

The ship was rolling heavily, and each time she went over, the wooden panelling on the walls creaked as if it were going to split. The passengers held on to the arms of their chairs, concentrating upon the auction.

"Low field!" the auctioneer called out. "The next number is low field."

Mr Botibol sat up very straight and tense. He would wait, he had decided, until the others had finished bidding, then he would jump in and make the last bid. He had figured that there must be at least five hundred dollars in his account at the bank at home, probably nearer six. That was about two hundred pounds – over two hundred. This ticket wouldn't fetch more than that.

"As you all know," the auctioneer was saying, "low field covers every number *below* the smallest number in the range, in this case every number below five hundred and five. So, if you think this ship is going to cover less than five hundred and five miles in the twenty-four hours ending at noon tomorrow, you better get in and buy this number. So what am I bid?"

It went clear up to one hundred and thirty pounds. Others besides Mr Botibol seemed to have noticed that the weather was rough. One hundred and forty . . . fifty . . . There it stopped. The auctioneer raised his hammer.

"Going at one hundred and fifty . . ."

"Sixty!" Mr Botibol called, and every face in the room turned and looked at him.

"Seventy!"

"Eighty!" Mr Botibol called.

"Ninety!"

"Two hundred!" Mr Botibol called. He wasn't stopping now – not for anyone.

There was a pause.

"Any advance on two hundred pounds?"

Sit still, he told himself. Sit absolutely still and don't look up. It's unlucky to look up. Hold your breath. No one's going to bid you up so long as you hold your breath.

"Going for two hundred pounds . . ." The auctioneer had a pink bald head and there were little beads of sweat sparkling on top of it. "Going . . ." Mr

Botibol held his breath. "Going . . . Gone!" The man banged the hammer on the table. Mr Botibol wrote out a cheque and handed it to the auctioneer's assistant, then he settled back in his chair to wait for the finish. He did not want to go to bed before he knew how much there was in the pool.

They added it up after the last number had been sold and it came to twenty-one hundred-odd pounds. That was around six thousand dollars. Ninety per cent to go to the winner, ten per cent to seamen's charities. Ninety per cent of six thousand was five thousand four hundred. Well – that was enough. He could buy the Lincoln convertible and there would be something left over, too. With this gratifying thought he went off, happy and excited, to his cabin.

When Mr Botibol awoke the next morning he lay quite still for several minutes with his eyes shut, listening for the sound of the gale, waiting for the roll of the ship. There was no sound of any gale and the ship was not rolling. He jumped up and peered out of the porthole. The sea – Oh Jesus God – was smooth as glass, the great ship was moving through it fast, obviously making up for time lost during the night. Mr Botibol turned away and sat slowly down on the edge of his bunk. A fine electricity of fear was beginning to prickle under the skin of his stomach. He hadn't a hope now. One of the higher numbers was certain to win it after this.

"Oh, my God," he said aloud. "What shall I do?"

What, for example, would Ethel say? It was simply not possible to tell her that he had spent almost all of their two years' savings on a ticket in the ship's pool. Nor was it possible to keep the matter secret. To do that he would have to tell her to stop drawing cheques. And what about the monthly instalments on the television set and the *Encyclopaedia Britannica*? Already he could see the anger and contempt in the woman's eyes, the blue becoming grey and the eyes themselves narrowing as they always did when there was anger in them.

"Oh, my God. What *shall* I do?"

There was no point in pretending that he had the slightest chance now – not unless the goddam ship started to go backwards. They'd have to put her in reverse and go full speed astern and keep right on going if he was to have any chance of winning it now. Well, maybe he should ask the captain to do just that. Offer him ten per cent of the profits. Offer him more if he wanted it. Mr Botibol started to giggle. Then very suddenly he stopped, his eyes and mouth both opening wide in a kind of shocked surprise. For it was at this moment that the idea came. It hit him hard and quick, and he jumped up from his bed, terribly excited, ran over to the porthole and looked out again. Well, he thought, why not? Why ever not? The sea was calm and he wouldn't have any trouble keeping afloat until they picked him up. He had a vague feeling that someone had done this thing before, but that didn't prevent him from doing it again. The ship would have to stop and lower a boat, and the boat would have to go back maybe half a mile to get him, and then it would have to return to the ship, the whole thing. An hour was about thirty miles. It would knock thirty miles off the day's run. That would do it. "Low field" would be sure to win it then. Just so long as he made certain someone saw him falling over; but that would be simple to arrange. And he'd better wear light clothes, something easy to swim in. Sports clothes, that was it. He would dress as though he were going up to play some deck tennis – just a shirt and a pair of shorts and tennis-shoes. And leave his watch behind. What was the time? Nine-fifteen. The sooner the better, then. Do it now and get it over with. Have to do it soon, because the time limit was midday.

Mr Botibol was both frightened and excited when he stepped out on to the sun deck in his sports clothes. His small body was wide at the hips, tapering upward to extremely narrow sloping shoulders, so that it resembled, in shape at any rate, a bollard. His white skinny legs were covered with black hairs, and he came cautiously out on deck, treading softly in his tennis shoes. Nervously he looked around him. There was only one other person in sight, an elderly woman with very thick ankles and immense buttocks who was leaning over the rail staring at the sea. She was wearing a coat of Persian lamb and the collar was turned up so Mr Botibol couldn't see her face.

He stood still, examining her carefully from a distance. Yes, he told himself, she would probably do. She would probably give the alarm just as quickly as anyone else. But wait one minute, take your time, William Botibol, take your time. Remember what you told yourself a few minutes ago in the cabin when you were changing? You remember that?

The thought of leaping off a ship into the ocean a thousand miles from the nearest land had made Mr Botibol – a cautious man at the best of times – unusually advertent. He was by no means satisfied yet that this woman he saw before him was *absolutely certain* to give the alarm when he made his jump. In his opinion there were two possible reasons why she might fail him. Firstly, she might be deaf and blind. It was not very probable, but on the other hand it *might* be so, and why take a chance? All he had to do was check it by talking to her for a moment beforehand. Secondly – and this will demonstrate how suspicious the mind of a man can become when it is working through self-preservation and fear – secondly, it had occurred to him that the woman might herself be the owner of one of the high numbers in the pool and as such would have a sound financial reason for not wishing to stop the ship. Mr Botibol recalled that people had killed their fellows for far less than six thousand dollars. It was happening every day in the newspapers. So why take a chance on that either? Check on it first. Be sure of your facts. Find out about it by a little polite conversation. Then, provided that the woman appeared also to be a pleasant, kindly human being, the thing was a cinch and he could leap overboard with a light heart.

Mr Botibol advanced casually towards the woman and took up a position beside her, leaning on the rail. "Hullo," he said pleasantly.

She turned and smiled at him, a surprisingly lovely, almost a beautiful smile, although the face itself was very plain. "Hullo," she answered him.

Check, Mr Botibol told himself, on the first question. She is neither blind nor deaf. "Tell me," he said, coming straight to the point, "what did you think of the auction last night?"

"Auction?" she asked, frowning. "Auction? What auction?"

"You know, that silly old thing they have in the lounge after dinner, selling numbers on the ship's daily run. I just wondered what you thought about it."

She shook her head, and again she smiled, a sweet and pleasant smile that had in it perhaps the trace of an apology. "I'm very lazy," she said. "I always go to bed early. I have my dinner in bed. It's so restful to have dinner in bed."

Mr Botibol smiled back at her and began to edge away. "Got to go and get my exercise now," he said. "Never miss my exercise in the morning. It was nice seeing you. Very nice seeing you . . ." He retreated about ten paces, and the woman let him go without looking around.

Everything was now in order. The sea was calm, he was lightly dressed for swimming, there were almost certainly no man-eating sharks in this part of the Atlantic, and there was this pleasant kindly old woman to give the alarm. It was a question now only of whether the ship would be delayed long enough to swing the balance in his favour. Almost certainly it would. In any event, he could do a little to help in that direction himself. He could make a few difficulties about getting hauled up into the lifeboat. Swim around a bit, back away from them surreptitiously as they tried to come up close to fish him out. Every

minute, every second gained would help him win. He began to move forward again to the rail, but now a new fear assailed him. Would he get caught in the propeller? He had heard about that happening to persons falling off the sides of big ships. But then, he wasn't going to fall, he was going to jump, and that was a
5 very different thing. Provided he jumped out far enough he would be sure to clear the propeller.

Mr Botibol advanced slowly to a position at the rail about twenty yards away from the woman. She wasn't looking at him now. So much the better. He didn't want her watching him as he jumped off. So long as no one was watching
10 he would be able to say afterwards that he had slipped and fallen by accident. He peered over the side of the ship. It was a long, long drop. Come to think of it now, he might easily hurt himself badly if he hit the water flat. Wasn't there someone who once split his stomach open that way, doing a belly flop from the high dive? He must jump straight and land feet first. Go in like a knife. Yes, sir.
15 The water seemed cold and deep and grey and it made him shiver to look at it. But it was now or never. Be a man, William Botibol, be a man. All right then . . . now . . . here goes . . .

He climbed up on to the wide wooden top-rail, stood there poised, balancing for three terrifying seconds, then he leaped – he leaped up and out as far as
20 he could go and at the same time he shouted *"Help!"*

"Help! Help!" he shouted as he fell. Then he hit the water and went under.

When the first shout for help sounded, the woman who was leaning on the rail started up and gave a little jump of surprise. She looked around quickly and saw sailing past her through the air this small man dressed in white shorts and
25 tennis shoes, spreadeagled and shouting as he went. For a moment she looked as though she weren't quite sure what she ought to do: throw a lifebelt, run away and give the alarm, or simply turn and yell. She drew back a pace from the rail and swung half around facing up to the bridge, and for this brief moment she remained motionless, tense, undecided. Then almost at once she seemed to
30 relax, and she leaned forward far over the rail, staring at the water where it was turbulent in the ship's wake. Soon a tiny round black head appeared in the foam, an arm was raised above it, once, twice, vigorously waving, and a small faraway voice was heard calling something that was difficult to understand. The woman leaned still farther over the rail, trying to keep the little bobbing
35 black speck in sight, but soon, so very soon, it was such a long way away that she couldn't even be sure it was there at all.

After a while another woman came out on deck. This one was bony and angular, and she wore horn-rimmed spectacles. She spotted the first woman and walked over to her, treading the deck in the deliberate, military fashion of all spinsters.

"So *there* you are," she said.

The woman with the fat ankles turned and looked at her, but said nothing.

"I've been searching for you," the bony one continued. "Searching all over."

"It's very odd," the woman with the fat ankles said. "A man dived overboard just now, with his clothes on."

"Nonsense!"

"Oh yes. He said he wanted to get some exercise and he dived in and didn't even bother to take his clothes off."

"You better come down now," the bony woman said. Her mouth had suddenly become firm, her whole face sharp and alert, and she spoke less kindly than before. "And don't you ever go wandering about on deck alone like this again. You know quite well you're meant to wait for me."

"Yes, Maggie," the woman with the fat ankles answered, and again she smiled, a tender, trusting smile, and she took the hand of the other one and allowed herself to be led away across the deck.

"Such a nice man," she said. "He waved to me."

Katherine Mansfield

The Doll's House

When dear old Mrs Hay went back to town after staying with the Burnells she sent the children a doll's house. It was so big that the carter and Pat carried it into the courtyard, and there it stayed, propped up on two wooden boxes beside the feed-room door. No harm could come to it; it was summer. And perhaps the smell of paint would have gone off by the time it had to be taken in. For, really, the smell of paint coming from that doll's house ("Sweet of old Mrs Hay, of course; most sweet and generous!") – but the smell of paint was quite enough to make anyone seriously ill, in Aunt Beryl's opinion. Even before the sacking was taken off. And when it was . . .

There stood the Doll's house, a dark, oily, spinach green, picked out with bright yellow. Its two solid little chimneys, glued on to the roof, were painted red and white, and the door, gleaming with yellow varnish, was like a little slab of toffee. Four windows, real windows, were divided into panes by a broad streak of green. There was actually a tiny porch, too, painted yellow, with big lumps of congealed paint hanging along the edge.

But perfect, perfect little house! Who could possibly mind the smell! It was part of the joy, part of the newness.

"Open it quickly, someone!"

The hook at the side was stuck fast. Pat prised it open with his penknife, and the whole house front swung back, and – there you were, gazing at one and the same moment into the drawing-room and dining-room, the kitchen and two bedrooms. That is the way for a house to open! Why don't all houses open like that? How much more exciting than peering through the slit of a door into a mean little hall with a hat-stand and two umbrellas! That is – isn't it? – what you long to know about a house when you put your hand on the knocker. Perhaps it is the way God opens houses at the dead of night when He is taking a quiet turn with an angel . . .

"O-oh!" The Burnell children sounded as though they were in despair. It was too marvellous; it was too much for them. They had never seen anything like it in their lives. All the rooms were papered. There were pictures on the walls, painted on the paper, with gold frames complete. Red carpet covered all the floors except the kitchen; red plush chairs in the drawing-room, green in the dining-room; tables, beds with real bed-clothes, a cradle, a stove, a dresser with plates and one big jug. But what Kezia liked more than anything, what she liked frightfully, was the lamp. It stood in the middle of the dining-room table, an exquisite little amber lamp with a white globe. It was even filled all ready for lighting, though, of course, you couldn't light it. But there was something inside that looked like oil and moved when you shook it.

The father and mother dolls, who sprawled very stiff as though they had fainted in the drawing-room, and their two little children asleep upstairs, were really too big for the doll's house. They didn't look as though they belonged. But the lamp was perfect. It seemed to smile at Kezia, to say, "I live here." The lamp was real.

The Burnell children could hardly walk to school fast enough the next morning. They burned to tell everybody, to describe, to – well – to boast about their doll's house before the school-bell rang.

"I'm to tell," said Isabel, "because I'm the eldest. And you two can join after. But I'm to tell first."

There was nothing to answer. Isabel was bossy, but she was always right, and Lottie and Kezia knew too well the powers that went with being eldest. They brushed through the thick buttercups at the road edge and said nothing.

"And I'm to choose who's to come and see it first. Mother said I might."

For it had been arranged that while the doll's house stood in the courtyard they might ask the girls at school, two at a time, to come and look. Not to stay to tea, of course, or to come traipsing through the house. But just to stand quietly in the courtyard while Isabel pointed out the beauties, and Lottie and Kezia looked pleased . . .

But hurry as they might, by the time they had reached the tarred palings of the boys' playground the bell had begun to jangle. They only just had time to whip off their hats and fall into line before the roll was called. Never mind. Isabel tried to make up for it by looking very important and mysterious and by whispering behind her hand to the girls near her, "Got something to tell you at playtime."

Playtime came and Isabel was surrounded. The girls of her class nearly fought to put their arms round her, to walk away with her, to beam flatteringly, to be her special friend. She held quite a court under the huge pine trees at the side of the playground. Nudging, giggling together, the little girls pressed up close. And the only two who stayed outside the ring were the two who were always outside, the little Kelveys. They knew better than to come anywhere near the Burnells.

5   For the fact was, the school the Burnell children went to was not at all the kind of place their parents would have chosen if there had been any choice. But there was none. It was the only school for miles. And the consequence was all the children of the neighbourhood, the Judge's little girls, the doctor's daughters, the storekeeper's children, the milkman's, were forced to mix together.
10 Not to speak of there being an equal number of rude, rough little boys as well. But the line had to be drawn somewhere. It was drawn at the Kelveys. Many of the children, including the Burnells, were not allowed even to speak to them. They walked past the Kelveys with their heads in the air, and as they set the fashion in all matters of behaviour, the Kelveys were shunned by everybody.
15 Even the teacher had a special voice for them, and a special smile for the other children when Lil Kelvey came up to her desk with a bunch of dreadfully common-looking flowers.

They were the daughters of a spry, hard-working little washerwoman, who went about from house to house by the day. This was awful enough. But where
20 was Mr Kelvey? Nobody knew for certain. But everybody said he was in prison. So they were the daughters of a washerwoman and a gaolbird. Very nice company for other people's children! And they looked it. Why Mrs Kelvey made them so conspicuous was hard to understand. The truth was they were dressed in "bits" given to her by the people for whom she worked. Lil, for
25 instance, who was a stout, plain child, with big freckles, came to school in a dress made from a green art-serge table-cloth of the Burnells', with red plush sleeves from the Logans' curtains. Her hat, perched on top of her high forehead, was a grown-up woman's hat, once the property of Miss Lecky, the postmistress. It was turned up at the back and trimmed with a large scarlet
30 quill. What a little guy she looked! It was impossible not to laugh. And her little sister, our Else, wore a long white dress, rather like a night-gown, and a pair of little boy's boots. But whatever our Else wore she would have looked strange. She was a tiny wish-bone of a child, with cropped hair and enormous solemn eyes – a little white owl. Nobody had ever seen her smile; she scarcely ever
35 spoke. She went through life holding on to Lil, with a piece of Lil's skirt screwed up in her hand. Where Lil went, our Else followed. In the playground,

on the road going to and from school, there was Lil marching in front and our Else holding on behind. Only when she wanted anything, or when she was out of breath, our Else gave Lil a tug, a twitch, and Lil stopped and turned round. The Kelveys never failed to understand each other.

Now they hovered at the edge; you couldn't stop them listening. When the little girls turned round and sneered, Lil, as usual, gave her silly, shamefaced smile, but our Else only looked.

And Isabel's voice, so very proud, went on telling. The carpet made a great sensation, but so did the beds with real bed-clothes, and the stove with an oven door.

When she finished, Kezia broke in. "You've forgotten the lamp, Isabel."

"Oh, yes," said Isabel, "and there's a teeny little lamp, all made of yellow glass, with a white globe that stands on the dining-room table. You couldn't tell it from a real one."

"The lamp's best of all," cried Kezia. She thought Isabel wasn't making half enough of the little lamp. But nobody paid any attention. Isabel was choosing the two who were to come back with them that afternoon and see it. She chose Emmie Cole and Lena Logan. But when the others knew they were all to have a chance, they couldn't be nice enough to Isabel. One by one they put their arms round Isabel's waist and walked her off. They had something to whisper to her, a secret. "Isabel's *my* friend."

Only the little Kelveys moved away forgotten; there was nothing more for them to hear.

Days passed, and as more children saw the doll's house, the fame of it spread. It became the one subject, the rage. The one question was, "Have you seen Burnells' doll's house? Oh, ain't it lovely!" "Haven't you seen it? Oh, I say!"

Even the dinner hour was given up to talking about it. The little girls sat under the pines eating their thick mutton sandwiches and big slabs of johnny cake spread with butter. While always, as near as they could get, sat the Kelveys, our Else holding on to Lil, listening too, while they chewed their jam sandwiches out of a newspaper soaked with large red blobs.

"Mother," said Kezia, "can't I ask the Kelveys just once?"

"Certainly not, Kezia."

"But why not?"

"Run away, Kezia; you know quite well why not."

At last everybody had seen it except them. On that day the subject rather flagged. It was the dinner hour. The children stood together under the pine trees, and suddenly, as they looked at the Kelveys eating out of their paper, always by themselves, always listening, they wanted to be horrid to them. Emmie Cole started the whisper.

"Lil Kelvey's going to be a servant when she grows up."

"O-oh, how awful!" said Isabel Burnell, and she made eyes at Emmie.

Emmie swallowed in a very meaning way and nodded to Isabel as she'd seen her mother do on those occasions.

"It's true – it's true – it's true," she said.

Then Lena Logan's little eyes snapped. "Shall I ask her?" she whispered.

"Bet you don't," said Jessie May.

"Pooh, I'm not frightened," said Lena. Suddenly she gave a little squeal and danced in front of the other girls. "Watch! Watch me! Watch me now!" said Lena. And sliding, gliding, dragging one foot, giggling behind her hand, Lena went over to the Kelveys.

Lil looked up from her dinner. She wrapped the rest quickly away. Our Else stopped chewing. What was coming now?

"Is it true you're going to be a servant when you grow up, Lil Kelvey?" shrilled Lena.

Dead silence. But instead of answering, Lil only gave her silly, shamefaced smile. She didn't seem to mind the question at all. What a sell for Lena! The girls began to titter.

Lena couldn't stand that. She put her hands on her hips; she shot forward. "Yah, yer father's in prison!" she hissed, spitefully.

This was such a marvellous thing to have said that the little girls rushed away in a body, deeply, deeply excited, wild with joy. Someone found a long rope, and they began skipping. And never did they skip so high, run in and out so fast, or do such daring things as on that morning.

In the afternoon Pat called for the Burnell children with the buggy and they drove home. There were visitors. Isabel and Lottie, who liked visitors, went upstairs to change their pinafores. But Kezia thieved out at the back. Nobody was about; she began to swing on the big white gates of the courtyard. Presently, looking along the road, she saw two little dots. They grew bigger, they were coming towards her. Now she could see that one was in front and one close behind. Now she could see that they were the Kelveys. Kezia stopped swinging.

She slipped off the gate as if she was going to run away. Then she hesitated. The Kelveys came nearer, and beside them walked their shadows, very long, stretching right across the road with their heads in the buttercups. Kezia clambered back on the gate; she had made up her mind; she swung out.

"Hullo," she said to the passing Kelveys.

They were so astounded that they stopped. Lil gave her silly smile. Our Else stared.

"You can come and see our doll's house if you want to," said Kezia, and she dragged one toe on the ground. But at that Lil turned red and shook her head quickly.

"Why not?" asked Kezia.

Lil gasped, then she said, "Your ma told our ma you wasn't to speak to us."

"Oh, well," said Kezia. She didn't know what to reply. "It doesn't matter. You can come and see our doll's house all the same. Come on. Nobody's looking."

But Lil shook her head still harder.

"Don't you want to?" asked Kezia.

Suddenly there was a twitch, a tug at Lil's skirt. She turned round. Our Else was looking at her with big, imploring eyes; she was frowning; she wanted to go. For a moment Lil looked at our Else very doubtfully. But then our Else twitched her skirt again. She started forward. Kezia led the way. Like two little stray cats they followed across the courtyard to where the doll's house stood.

"There it is," said Kezia.

There was a pause. Lil breathed loudly, almost snorted; our Else was still as stone.

"I'll open it for you," said Kezia kindly. She undid the hook and they looked inside.

"There's the drawing-room and the dining-room, and that's the . . ."

"Kezia!"

Oh, what a start they gave!

"Kezia!"

It was Aunt Beryl's voice. They turned round. At the back door stood Aunt Beryl, staring as if she couldn't believe what she saw.

"How dare you ask the little Kelveys into the courtyard?" said her cold, furious voice. "You know as well as I do, you're not allowed to talk to them. Run away, children, run away at once. And don't come back again," said Aunt

Beryl. And she stepped into the yard and shooed them out as if they were chickens.

"Off you go immediately!" she called, cold and proud.

They did not need telling twice. Burning with shame, shrinking together, Lil huddling along like her mother, our Else dazed, somehow they crossed the big courtyard and squeezed out of the white gate.

"Wicked, disobedient little girl!" said Aunt Beryl bitterly to Kezia, and she slammed the doll's house to.

The afternoon had been awful. A letter had come from Willie Brent, a terrifying, threatening letter, saying if she did not meet him that evening in Pulman's Bush, he'd come to the front door and ask the reason why! But now that she had frightened those little rats of Kelveys and given Kezia a good scolding, her heart felt lighter. That ghastly pressure was gone. She went back to the house humming.

When the Kelveys were well out of sight of Burnells', they sat down to rest on a big red drain-pipe by the side of the road. Lil's cheeks were still burning; she took off the hat with the quill and held it on her knee. Dreamily they looked over the hay paddocks, past the creek, to the group of wattles where Logan's cows stood waiting to be milked. What were their thoughts?

Presently our Else nudged up close to her sister. But now she had forgotten the cross lady. She put out a finger and stroked her sister's quill; she smiled her rare smile.

"I seen the little lamp," she said, softly.

Then both were silent once more.

Alun Lewis

The Lapse

At 4.13 Henry showed his season ticket to the porter and climbed into the railway car. He nodded politely to Miss Burge, the teacher at the kindergarten, who sat in her corner seat knitting the green jumper she had started last month; and to the district nurse in her black pork-pie hat, her professional bag tucked warmly against her stomach. They both smiled back – nothing said, never anything said – and he went to his usual place at the far end of the car. He filled his pipe while waiting for the train to start, and then put it back into his pocket.

Back and fore, back and fore, like a shuttle, workwards each morning, homewards each night, ra-ta-ta, ra-ta-ta, the train's travelling beat – how many times have I done this journey, these last five years? If I put the journeys end to end it would stretch a long way – right into Tibet perhaps, along the Turk-Sib, among the moujiks . . . Oh dear! Henry yawned and gazed indifferently at the row of slatternly back gardens and flapping clothes lines past which the train ran. Twice a day for five years, Bank holidays excepted, those drab hotchpotch backs where the wives riddled yesterday's ashes and the children sat on the steps eating bread and jam. It was so depressing to see those streets every day, always the same, and the people always the same – how many of them knew they had been condemned to serve a lifer?

And then, with a rattle and a wrench, the open country; the hills swooping like swallows. Below the embankment the black river swirled, wandering down from the coal mines at the head of the valley. And the train rattled over the bridge that spanned the river; Henry felt the drop under the bridge, sheer and empty in the pit of his stomach, like a bird flashing through a hollow cave. And on, accelerando, through the cutting. What shall I do tonight, the tired voice asked in his head. Pictures? Or a nap and a stroll down to the billiard hall? I don't know what to do, I can never make up my mind. I know what'll happen – I'll stand by my bedroom window looking down into the empty street. And in the end I won't go out. I'll waste the night, as usual, as I waste everything. I ought to decide to *do* something, to get *on* . . . One day I *will* do something, to justify all this waste, something grand, careless . . . I *must* . . .

I wonder what's for dinner this evening. Mother will have it all ready, whatever it is, warmed up and waiting; and she'll sit opposite me while I eat it, watching me wolf it; and at the end she'll have a cup of tea with me . . . Doctor said she's alright. But often I dream she is dead, and I wake up sweating.

Halt number one. The schoolgirl comes in and sits where she always sits, and takes a book out of her satchel, a different book this week. She has grown a lot in the last five years. She used to be a scrimpy, flat-chested little thing, her head always poked out of the window; now she sits absorbed in her book and there is a difference about everything she does. She must be about sixteen; she hardly looks it, with her mouse-bitten fringe and her black stockings. She's got a strange face; those who don't know her would never call it pretty. They'd only see her prominent top teeth, her weak chin, her flat cheekbones. They'd miss the secret quality, the look she has when she turns from her book to look out through the window. She's pulling on her woollen gloves; she gets out at the next halt. I wish I knew where she lives – in the semi-detached red-roofed houses on the right, or the huddle of slums on the left? Not that it matters really; the train always starts off before she's left the platform. Sometimes, if she hasn't finished her chapter before the train stops, she walks along the platform with her book open . . .

The little woman who only travels on Thursdays is snoring; she always puts her feet up and snoozes. Her head hangs forward, her oak-apple nose nearly dropping into her shopping basket, her pink umbrella laid across her lap. Her shoes need soling. Oh, curse it and curse it. It's always, always the same, daunting you properly. Makes you want to smash the window, pull the communication cord, scream . . . And instead you swallow the scream; you can hear it struggling inside you, battering at the door of your throat. And you sit still, and look at the old lady's brown hat, and Miss Burge knitting, and *her* reading. It's been lovely, really, watching her grow up, wondering about her, her name and what she thinks when she's reading and what Life will do to her, and feeling sorry for her, somehow . . .

The train stopped with a shudder that rattled all the windows. The red roofs and the biscuit facades of the new houses waited faithfully outside. The girl closed her book and obediently went out.

And then, all of a sudden, Henry got up and walked down the car, past Miss Burge and the district nurse, who stared at him in astonishment. The blood was beating like a steel hammer behind his eyes. He fumbled and tugged at the carriage door. But he got out, and was standing on the ash platform, for the first

time, ever. She was a few yards ahead of him, finishing her chapter, walking slowly, unaware. He stepped forward. The porter shouted "O.K." to the guard. The engine-driver leaned over the footplate. Henry stood stock still, looking at the girl, at the railings, at the yellow advertisement of Duck, Son and
5 Pinker's pianos. The guard shouted "What are you getting off here for?" The green flag and the engine's hoot . . . Henry scrambled back into the carriage, the guard shouted at him and a porter blasphemed. He shut the door with quivering hands and slouched back to his seat. Miss Burge and the nurse stared at him and at each other. He didn't notice anything. He just slumped into his seat and
10 clenched his hands, squeezing them between his knees. After a couple of minutes he blew his nose hard and rubbed some smuts out of his eyes. The train crashed into the black mouth of the tunnel with a shriek. It woke the old lady. She opened her eyes and tidied her collar, as if it were the most natural thing in the world to open one's eyes, after they had been closed.
15   The train came out of the tunnel and stopped. The old lady picked up her basket and her pink umbrella, Miss Burge rolled up her knitting, the nurse fingered the silver hatpin that skewered her pork-pie hat. Henry followed them out onto the platform and slunk past the guard like a criminal.

James Joyce

Eveline

She sat at the window watching the evening invade the avenue. Her head was leaned against the window curtains, and in her nostrils was the odour of dusty cretonne. She was tired.

Few people passed. The man out of the last house passed on his way home; she heard his footsteps clacking along the concrete pavement and afterwards crunching on the cinder path before the new red houses. One time there used to be a field there in which they used to play every evening with other people's children. Then a man from Belfast bought the field and built houses in it – not like their little brown houses, but bright brick houses with shining roofs. The children of the avenue used to play together in that field – the Devines, the Waters, the Dunns, little Keogh the cripple, she and her brothers and sisters. Ernest, however, never played: he was too grown up. Her father used often to hunt them in out of the field with his blackthorn stick; but usually little Keogh used to keep *nix* and call out when he saw her father coming. Still they seemed to have been rather happy then. Her father was not so bad then; and besides, her mother was alive. That was a long time ago; she and her brothers and sisters were all grown up; her mother was dead. Tizzie Dunn was dead, too, and the Waters had gone back to England. Everything changes. Now she was going to go away like the others, to leave her home.

Home! She looked round the room, reviewing all its familiar objects which she had dusted once a week for so many years, wondering where on earth all the dust came from. Perhaps she would never see again those familiar objects from which she had never dreamed of being divided. And yet during all those years she had never found out the name of the priest whose yellowing photograph hung on the wall above the broken harmonium beside the coloured print of the promises made to Blessed Margaret Mary Alacoque. He had been a school friend of her father. Whenever he showed the photograph to a visitor her father used to pass it with a casual word:

"He is in Melbourne now."

She had consented to go away, to leave her home. Was that wise? She tried to weigh each side of the question. In her home anyway she had shelter and food;

she had those whom she had known all her life about her. Of course she had to work hard, both in the house and at business. What would they say of her in the Stores when they found out that she had run away with a fellow? Say she was a fool, perhaps; and her place would be filled up by advertisement. Miss Gavan would be glad. She had always had an edge on her, especially whenever there were people listening.

"Miss Hill, don't you see these ladies are waiting?"

"Look lively, Miss Hill, please."

She would not cry many tears at leaving the Stores.

But in her new home, in a distant unknown country, it would not be like that. Then she would be married – she, Eveline. People would treat her with respect then. She would not be treated as her mother had been. Even now, though she was over nineteen, she sometimes felt herself in danger of her father's violence. She knew it was that that had given her the palpitations. When they were growing up he had never gone for her, like he used to go for Harry and Ernest, because she was a girl; but latterly he had begun to threaten her and say what he would do to her only for her dead mothers's sake. And now she had nobody to protect her, Ernest was dead and Harry, who was in the church decorating business, was nearly always down somewhere in the country. Besides, the invariable squabble for money on Saturday nights had begun to weary her unspeakably. She always gave her entire wages – seven shillings – and Harry always sent up what he could, but the trouble was to get any money from her father. He said she used to squander the money, that she had no head, that he wasn't going to give her his hard-earned money to throw about the streets, and much more, for he was usually fairly bad on Saturday night. In the end he would give her the money and ask her had she any intention of buying Sunday's dinner. Then she had to rush out as quickly as she could and do her marketing, holding her black leather purse tightly in her hand as she elbowed her way through the crowds and returning home late under her load of provisions. She had hard work to keep the house together and to see that the two young children who had been left to her charge went to school regularly and got their meals regularly. It was hard work – a hard life – but now that she was about to leave it she did not find it a wholly undesirable life.

She was about to explore another life with Frank. Frank was very kind, manly, open-hearted. She was to go away with him by the night-boat to be his wife and to live with him in Buenos Ayres, where he had a home waiting for her.

How well she remembered the first time she had seen him; he was lodging in a house on the main road where she used to visit. It seemed a few weeks ago. He was standing at the gate, his peaked cap pushed back on his head and his hair tumbled forward over a face of bronze. Then they had come to know each other. He used to meet her outside the Stores every evening and see her home. He took her to see *The Bohemian Girl* and she felt elated as she sat in an unaccustomed part of the theatre with him. He was awfully fond of music and sang a little. People knew that they were courting, and, when he sang about the lass that loves a sailor, she always felt pleasantly confused. He used to call her Poppens out of fun. First of all it had been an excitement for her to have a fellow and then she had begun to like him. He had tales of distant countries. He had started as a deck boy at a pound a month on a ship of the Allan Line going out to Canada. He told her the names of the ships he had been on and the names of the different services. He had sailed through the Straits of Magellan and he told her stories of the terrible Patagonians. He had fallen on his feet in Buenos Ayres, he said, and had come over to the old country just for a holiday. Of course, her father had found out the affair and had forbidden her to have anything to say to him.

"I know these sailor chaps," he said.

One day he had quarrelled with Frank, and after that she had to meet her lover secretly.

The evening deepened in the avenue. The white of two letters in her lap grew indistinct. One was to Harry; the other was to her father. Ernest had been her favourite, but she liked Harry too. Her father was becoming old lately, she noticed; he would miss her. Sometimes he could be very nice. Not long before, when she had been laid up for a day, he had read her out a ghost story and made toast for her at the fire. Another day, when their mother was alive, they had all gone for a picnic to the Hill of Howth. She remembered her father putting on her mother's bonnet to make the children laugh.

Her time was running out, but she continued to sit by the window, leaning her head against the window curtain, inhaling the odour of dusty cretonne. Down far in the avenue she could hear a street organ playing. She knew the air. Strange that it should come that very night to remind her of the promise to her mother, her promise to keep the home together as long as she could. She remembered the last night of her mother's illness; she was again in the close, dark room at the other side of the hall and outside she heard a melancholy air of

Italy. The organ-player had been ordered to go away and given sixpence. She remembered her father strutting back into the sick-room saying:

"Damned Italians! coming over here!"

As she mused the pitiful vision of her mother's life laid its spell on the very quick of her being – that life of commonplace sacrifices closing in final craziness. She trembled as she heard again her mother's voice saying constantly with foolish insistence:

"Derevaun Seraun! Derevaun Seraun!"

She stood up in a sudden impulse of terror. Escape! She must escape! Frank would save her. He would give her life, perhaps love, too. But she wanted to live. Why should she be unhappy? She had a right to happiness. Frank would take her in his arms, fold her in his arms. He would save her.

She stood among the swaying crowd in the station at the North Wall. He held her hand and she knew that he was speaking to her, saying something about the passage over and over again. The station was full of soldiers with brown baggages. Through the wide doors of the sheds she caught a glimpse of the black mass of the boat, lying in beside the quay wall, with illumined portholes. She answered nothing. She felt her cheek pale and cold and, out of a maze of distress, she prayed to God to direct her, to show her what was her duty. The boat blew a long mournful whistle into the mist. If she went, tomorrow she would be on the sea with Frank, steaming towards Buenos Ayres. Their passage had been booked. Could she still draw back after all he had done for her? Her distress awoke a nausea in her body and she kept moving her lips in silent fervent prayer.

A bell clanged upon her heart. She felt him seize her hand:

"Come!"

All the seas of the world tumbled about her heart. He was drawing her into them: he would drown her. She gripped with both hands at the iron railing.

"Come!"

No! No! No! It was impossible. Her hands clutched the iron in frenzy. Amid the seas she sent a cry of anguish.

"Eveline! Evvy!"

He rushed beyond the barrier and called to her to follow. He was shouted at to go on, but he still called to her. She set her white face to him, passive, like a helpless animal. Her eyes gave him no sign of love or farewell or recognition.

Alan Sillitoe

On Saturday Afternoon

I once saw a bloke try to kill himself. I'll never forget the day because I was sitting in the house one Saturday afternoon, feeling black and fed up because everybody in the family had gone to the pictures, except me who'd for some reason been left out of it. 'Course, I didn't know then that I would soon see something you can never see in the same way on the pictures, a real bloke stringing himself up. I was only a kid at the time, so you can imagine how much I enjoyed it.

I've never known a family to look as black as our family when they're fed up. I've seen the old man with his face so dark and full of murder because he ain't got no fags or was having to use saccharine to sweeten his tea, or even for nothing at all, that I've backed out of the house in case he got up from his fireside chair and came for me. He just sits, almost on top of the fire, his oil-stained Sunday-joint maulers opened out in front of him and facing inwards to each other, his thick shoulders scrunched forward, and his dark brown eyes staring into the fire. Now and again he'd say a dirty word, for no reason at all, the worst word you can think of, and when he starts saying this you know it's time to clear out. If mam's in it gets worse than ever, because she says sharp to him: "What are yo' looking so bleddy black for?" as if it might be because of something she's done, and before you know what's happening he's tipped up a tableful of pots and mam's gone out of the house crying. Dad hunches back over the fire and goes on swearing. All because of a packet of fags.

I once saw him broodier than I'd ever seen him, so that I thought he'd gone crackers in a quiet sort of way – until a fly flew to within a yard of him. Then his hand shot out, got it, and slung it crippled into the roaring fire. After that he cheered up a bit and mashed some tea.

Well, that's where the rest of us get our black looks from. It stands to reason we'd have them with a dad who carries on like that, don't it? Black looks run in the family. Some families have them and some don't. Our family has them right enough, and that's certain, so when we're fed up we're really fed up. Nobody knows why we get as fed up as we do or why it gives us these black looks when we are. Some people get fed up and don't look bad at all: they seem happy in a

funny sort of way, as if they've just been set free from clink after being in there for something they didn't do, or come out of the pictures after sitting plugged for eight hours at a bad film, or just missed a bus they ran half a mile for and seen it was the wrong one just after they'd stopped running – but in our family
5 it's murder for the others if one of us is fed up. I've asked myself lots of times what it is, but I can never get any sort of answer even if I sit and think for hours, which I must admit I don't do, though it looks good when I say I do. But I sit and think for long enough, until mam says to me, at seeing me scrunched up over the fire like dad: "What are yo' looking so black for?" So I've just got to
10 stop thinking about it in case I get really black and fed up and go the same way as dad, tipping up a tableful of pots and all.

Mostly I suppose there's nothing to look so black for: though it's nobody's fault and you can't blame anyone for looking black because I'm sure it's summat in the blood. But on this Saturday afternoon I was looking so black that
15 when dad came in from the bookie's he said to me: "What's up wi' yo'?"

"I feel badly," I fibbed. He'd have had a fit if I'd said I was only black because I hadn't gone to the pictures.

"Well have a wash," he told me.

"I don't want a wash," I said, and that was a fact.

20 "Well, get outside and get some fresh air then," he shouted.

I did as I was told, double-quick, because if ever dad goes as far as to tell me to get some fresh air I know it's time to get away from him. But outside the air wasn't so fresh, what with that bloody great bike factory bashing away at the yard-end. I didn't know where to go, so I walked up the yard a bit and sat down
25 near somebody's back gate.

Then I saw this bloke who hadn't lived long in our yard. He was tall and thin and had a face like a parson except that he wore a flat cap and had a moustache that drooped, and looked as though he hadn't had a square meal for a year. I didn't think much o' this at the time: but I remember that as he turned in by the
30 yard-end one of the nosy gossiping women who stood there every minute of the day except when she trudged to the pawnshop with her husband's bike or best suit, shouted to him: "What's that rope for, mate?"

He called back: "It's to 'ang messen wi', missis," and she cackled at his bloody good joke so loud and long you'd think she never heard such a good
35 'un, though the next day she cackled on the other side of her fat face.

He walked by me puffing a fag and carrying his coil of brand-new rope, and he had to step over me to get past. His boot nearly took my shoulder off, and when I told him to watch where he was going I don't think he heard me because he didn't even look round. Hardly anybody was about. All the kids were still at the pictures, and most of their mams and dads were downtown doing the shopping.

The bloke walked down the yard to his back door, and having nothing better to do because I hadn't gone to the pictures I followed him. You see, he left his back door open a bit, so I gave it a push and went in. I stood there, just watching him, sucking my thumb, the other hand in my pocket. I suppose he knew I was there, because his eyes were moving more natural now, but he didn't seem to mind. "What are yer going to do wi' that rope, mate?" I asked him.

"I'm going ter 'ang messen, lad," he told me, as though he'd done it a time or two already, and people had usually asked him questions like this beforehand.

"What for mate?" He must have thought I was a nosy young bogger.

"'Cause I want to, that's what for," he said, clearing all the pots off the table and pulling it to the middle of the room. Then he stood on it to fasten the rope to the light-fitting. The table creaked and didn't look very safe, but it did him for what he wanted.

"It wain't hold up, mate," I said to him, thinking how much better it was being here than sitting in the pictures and seeing the Jungle Jim serial.

But he got nettled now and turned on me. "Mind yer own business."

I thought he was going to tell me to scram, but he didn't. He made ever such a fancy knot with that rope, as though he'd been a sailor or summat, and as he tied it he was whistling a fancy tune to himself. Then he got down from the table and pushed it back to the wall, and put a chair in its place. He wasn't looking black at all, nowhere near as black as anybody in our family when they're feeling fed up. If ever he'd looked only half as black as our dad looked twice a week he'd have hanged himself years ago, I couldn't help thinking. But he was making a good job of that rope all right, as though he'd thought about it a lot anyway, and as though it was going to be the last thing he'd ever do. But I knew something he didn't know, because he wasn't standing where I was. I knew the rope wouldn't hold up, and I told him so, again.

"Shut yer gob," he said, but quiet like, "or I'll kick yer out."

I didn't want to miss it, so I said nothing. He took his cap off and put it on the dresser, then he took his coat off, and his scarf, and spread them out on the sofa. I wasn't a bit frightened, like I might be now at sixteen, because it was interesting. And being only ten I'd never had a chance to see a bloke hang himself before. We got pally, the two of us, before he slipped the rope around his neck.

"Shut the door," he asked me, and I did as I was told. "Ye're a good lad for your age," he said to me while I sucked my thumb, and he felt in his pockets and pulled out all that was inside, throwing the handful of bits and bobs on the table: fag-packet and peppermints, a pawn-ticket, an old comb, and a few coppers. He picked out a penny and gave it to me, saying: "Now listen ter me, young 'un. I'm going to 'ang messen, and when I'm swinging I want you to gi' this chair a bloody good kick and push it away. All right?"

I nodded.

He put the rope around his neck, and then took it off like it was a tie that didn't fit. "What are yer going to do it for, mate?" I asked again.

"Because I'm fed up," he said, looking very unhappy. "And because I want to. My missus left me, and I'm out o' work."

I didn't want to argue, because the way he said it, I knew he couldn't do anything else except hang himself. Also there was a funny look in his face: even when he talked to me I swear he couldn't see me. It was different to the black looks my old man puts on, and I suppose that's why my old man would never hang himself, worse luck, because he never gets a look into his clock like this bloke had. My old man's look stares *at* you, so that you have to back down and fly out of the house: this bloke's look looked *through* you, so that you could face it and know it wouldn't do you any harm. So I saw now that dad would never hang himself because he could never get the right sort of look into his face, in spite of the fact that he'd been out of work often enough. Maybe mam would have to leave him first, and then he might do it; but no – I shook my head – there wasn't much chance of that even though he did lead her a dog's life.

"Yer wain't forget to kick that chair away?" he reminded me, and I swung my head to say I wouldn't. So my eyes were popping and I watched every move he made. He stood on the chair and put the rope around his neck so that it fitted this time, still whistling his fancy tune. I wanted to get a better goz at the knot, because my pal was in the scouts, and would ask to know how it was done, and if I told him later he'd let me know what happened at the pictures in the Jungle Jim serial, so's I could have my cake and eat it as well, as mam says, tit for tat. But I thought I'd better not ask the bloke to tell me, and I stayed back in my corner. The last thing he did was take the wet dirty butt-end from his lips and sling it into the empty firegrate, following it with his eyes to the black fireback where it landed – as if he was then going to mend a fault in the lighting like any electrician.

Suddenly his long legs wriggled and his feet tried to kick the chair, so I helped him as I'd promised I would and took a runner at it as if I was playing centre-forward for Notts Forest, and the chair went scooting back against the sofa, dragging his muffler to the floor as it tipped over. He swung for a bit, his arms chafing like he was a scarecrow flapping birds away, and he made a noise in his throat as if he'd just took a dose of salts and was trying to make them stay down.

Then there was another sound, and I looked up and saw a big crack come in the ceiling, like you see on the pictures when an earthquake's happening, and the bulb began circling round and round as though it was a space ship. I was just beginning to get dizzy when, thank Christ, he fell down, with such a horrible thump on the floor that I thought he'd broke every bone he'd got. He kicked around for a bit, like a dog that's got colic bad. Then he lay still.

I didn't stay to look at him. "I told him that rope wouldn't hold up," I kept saying to myself as I went out of the house, tut-tutting because he hadn't done the job right, hands stuffed deep into my pockets and nearly crying at the balls-up he'd made of everything. I slammed his gate so hard with disappointment that it nearly dropped off its hinges.

Just as I was going back up the yard to get my tea at home, hoping the others had come back from the pictures so's I wouldn't have anything to keep on being black about, a copper passed me and headed for the bloke's door. He was striding quickly with his head bent forward, and I knew that somebody had narked. They must have seen him buy the rope and then tipped off the cop. Or happen the old hen at the yard-end had finally caught on. Or perhaps he'd even told somebody himself, because I supposed that the bloke who'd strung himself up hadn't much known what he was doing, especially with the look I'd seen in his eyes. But that's how it is, I said to myself, as I followed the copper back to the bloke's house, a poor bloke can't even hang himself these days.

When I got back the copper was slitting the rope from his neck with a penknife, then he gave him a drink of water, and the bloke opened his peepers. I didn't like the copper, because he'd got a couple of my mates sent to approved school for pinching lead piping from lavatories.

"What did you want to hang yourself for?" he asked the bloke, trying to make him sit up. He could hardly talk, and one of his hands was bleeding from where the light-bulb had smashed. I knew that rope wouldn't hold up, but he hadn't listened to me. I'll never hang myself anyway, but if I want to I'll make sure I do it from a tree or something like that, not a light fitting. "Well, what did you do it for?"

"Because I wanted to," the bloke croaked.

"You'll get five years for this," the copper told him. I'd crept back into the house and was sucking my thumb in the same corner.

"That's what yo' think," the bloke said, a normal frightened look in his eyes now. "I only wanted to hang myself."

"Well," the copper said, taking out his book, "it's against the law, you know."

"Nay," the bloke said, "it can't be. It's my life, ain't it?"

"You might think so," the copper said, "but it ain't."

He began to suck the blood from his hand. It was such a little scratch though that you couldn't see it. "That's the first thing I knew," he said.

"Well I'm telling you," the copper told him.

'Course, I didn't let on to the copper that I'd helped the bloke to hang himself. I wasn't born yesterday, nor the day before yesterday either.

"It's a fine thing if a bloke can't tek his own life," the bloke said, seeing he was in for it.

"Well he can't," the copper said, as if reading out of his book and enjoying it. "It ain't your life. And it's a crime to take your own life. It's killing yourself. It's suicide."

The bloke looked hard, as if every one of the copper's words meant six-months cold. I felt sorry for him, and that's a fact, but if only he'd listened to what I'd said and not depended on that light-fitting. He should have done it from a tree, or something like that.

He went up the yard with the copper like a peaceful lamb, and we all thought that that was the end of that.

But a couple of days later the news was flashed through to us – even before it got to the *Post* because a woman in our yard worked at the hospital of an evening dishing grub out and tidying up. I heard her spilling it to somebody at the yard-end. "I'd never 'ave thought it. I thought he'd got that daft idea out of his head when they took him away. But no. Wonders'll never cease. Chucked 'issen from the hospital window when the copper who sat near his bed went off for a pee. Would you believe it? Dead? Not much 'e ain't."

He'd heaved himself at the glass, and fallen like a stone on to the road. In one way I was sorry he'd done it, but in another I was glad, because he'd proved to the coppers and everybody whether it was his life or not all right. It was marvellous though, the way the brainless bastards had put him in a ward six floors up, which finished him off, proper, even better than a tree.

All of which will make me think twice about how black I sometimes feel. The black coal-bag locked inside you, and the black look it puts on your face, doesn't mean you're going to string yourself up or sling yourself under a double-decker or chuck yourself out of a window or cut your throat with a sardine-tin or put your head in the gas-oven or drop your rotten sack-bag of a body on to a railway line, because when you're feeling that black you can't even move from your chair. Anyhow, I know I'll never get so black as to hang myself, because hanging don't look very nice to me, and never will, the more I remember old what's-his-name swinging from the light-fitting.

More than anything else, I'm glad now I didn't go to the pictures that Saturday afternoon when I was feeling black and ready to do myself in. Because you know, I shan't ever kill myself. Trust me. I'll stay alive half-barmy till I'm a hundred and five, and then go out screaming blue murder because I want to stay where I am.

John Wain

A Message from the Pig-Man

He was never called Ekky now, because he was getting to be a real boy, nearly six, with grey flannel trousers that had a separate belt and weren't kept up by elastic, and his name was Eric. But this was just one of those changes brought about naturally, by time, not a disturbing alteration; he understood that. His mother hadn't meant that kind of change, when she had promised, "Nothing will be changed." It was all going to go on as before, except that Dad wouldn't be there, and Donald would be there instead. He knew Donald, of course, and felt all right about his being in the house, though it seemed, when he lay in bed and thought about it, mad and pointless that Donald's coming should mean that Dad had to go. Why should it mean that? The house was quite big. He hadn't any brothers and sisters, and if he *had* had any he wouldn't have minded sharing his bedroom, even with a baby that wanted a lot of looking after, so long as it left the spare room free for Dad to sleep in. If he did that, they wouldn't have a spare room, it was true, but then, the spare room was nearly always empty; the last time anybody had used the spare room was *years* ago, when he had been much smaller – last winter, in fact. And, even then, the visitor, the lady with the funny teeth who laughed as she breathed in, instead of as she breathed out like everyone else, had only stayed two or three nights. *Why* did grown-ups do everything in such a mad, silly way? They often told him not to be silly, but they were silly themselves in a useless way, not laughing or singing or anything, just being silly and sad.

It was so hard to read the signs; that was another thing. When they did give you something to go on, it was impossible to know how to take it. Dad had bought him a train, just a few weeks ago, and taught him how to fit the lines together. That ought to have meant that he would stay; what sensible person would buy a train, and fit it all up ready to run, even as a present for another person – *and then leave*? Donald had been quite good about the train, Eric had to admit that; he had bought a bridge for it and a lot of rolling-stock. At first he had got the wrong kind of rolling-stock, with wheels too close together to fit on to the rails; but instead of playing the usual grown-ups' trick of pulling a face and then not doing anything about it, he had gone back to the shop, straight away that same afternoon, and got the right kind. Perhaps that meant *he* was going to leave. But that didn't seem likely. Not the way Mum held on to him all the time, even holding him round the middle as if he needed keeping in one piece.

All the same, he was not Ekky now, he was Eric, and he was sensible and grown-up. Probably it was his own fault that everything seemed strange. He was not living up to his grey flannel trousers – perhaps that was it; being afraid of too many things, not asking questions that would probably turn out to have quite simple answers.

The Pig-man for instance. He had let the Pig-man worry him far too much. None of the grown-ups acted as if the Pig-man was anything to be afraid of. He probably just *looked* funny, that was all. If, instead of avoiding him so carefully, he went outside one evening and looked at him, took a good long, unafraid look, leaving the back door open behind him so that he could dart in to the safety and warmth of the house . . . no! It was better, after all, not to see the Pig-man; not till he was bigger, anyway; nearly six was quite big but it wasn't really *very* big . . .

And yet it was one of those puzzling things. No one ever told him to be careful not to let the Pig-man get hold of him, or warned him in any way; so the Pig-man *must* be harmless, because when it came to anything that *could* hurt you, like the traffic on the main road, people were always ramming it into you that you must look both ways, and all that stuff. And yet when it came to the Pig-man, no one ever mentioned him: he seemed beneath the notice of grown-ups. His mother would say, now and then, "Let me see, it's today the Pig-man comes, isn't it?" or, "Oh dear, the Pig-man will be coming round soon, and I haven't put anything out." If she talked like this, Eric's spine would tingle and go cold; he would keep very still and wait, because quite often her next words would be, "Eric, just take these peelings," or whatever it was, "out to the bucket, dear, will you?" The bucket was about fifty yards away from the back door; it was shared by the people in the two next-door houses. None of *them* was afraid of the Pig-man, either. What was their attitude, he wondered? Were they sorry for him, having to eat damp old stuff out of a bucket – tea-leaves and eggshells and that sort of thing? Perhaps he cooked it when he got home, and made it a bit nicer. Certainly, it didn't look too nice when you lifted the lid of the bucket and saw it all lying there. It sometimes smelt, too. Was the Pig-man very poor? Was he sorry for himself, or did he feel all right about being like that? *Like what?* What did the Pig-man look like? He would have little eyes, and a snout with a flat end; but would he have trotters, or hands and feet like a person's?

Lying on his back, Eric worked soberly at the problem. The Pig-man's bucket had a handle; so he must carry it in the ordinary way, in his hand – unless, of course, he walked on all fours and carried it in his mouth. But that wasn't very likely, because if he walked on all fours, what difference would there be between him and an ordinary pig? To be called the Pig-man, rather than the Man-pig, surely implied that he was upright, and dressed. Could he talk? Probably, in a kind of grunting way, or else how could he tell the people what kind of food he wanted them to put in his bucket? *Why hadn't he asked Dad about the Pig-man?* That had been his mistake; Dad would have told him exactly all about it. But he had gone. Eric fell asleep, and in his sleep he saw Dad and the Pig-man going in a train together; he called, but they did not hear and the train carried them away. "Dad!" he shouted desperately after it. "Don't bring the Pig-man when you come back! Don't bring the Pig-man!" Then his mother was in the room, kissing him and smelling nice; she felt soft, and the softness ducked him into sleep, this time without dreams; but the next day his questions returned.

Still, there was school in the morning, and going down to the swings in the afternoon, and altogether a lot of different things to crowd out the figure of the Pig-man and the questions connected with it. And he was never further from worrying about it all than that moment, a few evenings later, when it suddenly came to a crisis.

Eric had been allowed, "just for once," to bring his train into the dining-room after tea, because there was a fire there that made it nicer than the room where he usually played. It was warm and bright, and the carpet in front of the fireplace was smooth and firm, exactly right for laying out the rails on. Donald had come home and was sitting – in Dad's chair, but never mind – reading the paper and smoking. Mum was in the kitchen, clattering gently about, and both doors were open so that she and Donald could call out remarks to each other. Only a short passage lay between. It was just the part of the day Eric liked best, and bed-time was comfortably far off. He fitted the sections of rail together, glancing in anticipation at the engine as it stood proudly waiting to haul the carriages round and round, tremendously fast.

Then his mother called, "Eric! Do be a sweet, good boy, and take this stuff out for the Pig-man. My hands are covered with cake mixture. I'll let you scrape out the basin when you come in."

For a moment he kept quite still, hoping he hadn't really heard her say it, that it was just a voice inside his head. But Donald looked over at him and said, "Go along, old man. You don't mind, do you?"

Eric said, "But tonight's when the Pig-man *comes*."

Surely, *surely* they weren't asking him to go out, in the deep twilight, just at the time when there was the greatest danger of actually *meeting* the Pig-man?

"All the better," said Donald, turning back to his paper.

Why was it better? Did they *want* him to meet the Pig-man?

Slowly, wondering why his feet and legs didn't refuse to move, Eric went through into the kitchen. "There it is," his mother said, pointing to a brown-paper carrier full of potato-peelings and scraps.

He took it up and opened the back door. If he was quick, and darted along to the bucket *at once,* he would be able to lift the lid, throw the stuff in quickly, and be back in the house in about the time it took to count ten.

One – two – three – four – five – six. He stopped. The bucket wasn't there.

It had gone. Eric peered round, but the light, though faint, was not as faint as *that*. He could see that the bucket had gone. *The Pig-man had already been.*

Seven – eight – nine – ten, his steps were joyous and light. Back in the house, where it was warm and bright and his train was waiting.

"The Pig-man's gone, Mum. The bucket's not there."

She frowned, hands deep in the pudding-basin. "Oh, yes, I do believe I heard him. But it was only a moment ago. Yes, it was just before I called you, darling. It must have been that that made me think of it."

"Yes?" he said politely, putting down the carrier.

"So if you nip along, dear, you can easily catch him up. And I *do* want that stuff out of the way."

"Catch him up?" he asked, standing still in the doorway.

"Yes, dear, *catch him up,*" she answered rather sharply (the Efficient Young Mother knows when to be Firm). "He can't possibly be more than a very short way down the road."

Before she had finished Eric was outside the door and running. This was a technique he knew. It was the same as getting into icy cold water. If it was the end, if the Pig-man seized him by the hand and dragged him off to his hut, well, so much the worse. Swinging the paper carrier in his hand, he ran fast through the dusk.

The back view of the Pig-man was much as he had expected it to be. A slow, rather lurching gait, hunched shoulders, an old hat crushed down on his head (to hide his ears?) and the pail in his hand. Plod, plod, as if he were tired. Perhaps this was just a ruse, though, probably he could pounce quickly enough when his wicked little eyes saw a nice tasty little boy or something . . . did the Pig-man eat birds? Or cats?

Eric stopped. He opened his mouth to call to the Pig-man, but the first time he tried, nothing came out except a small rasping squeak. His heart was banging like fireworks going off. He could hardly hear anything.

"Mr Pig-man!" he called, and this time the words came out clear and rather high.

The jogging old figure stopped, turned, and looked at him. Eric could not see properly from where he stood. But he *had* to see. Everything, even his fear, sank and drowned in the raging tide of his curiosity. He moved forward. With each step he saw more clearly. The Pig-man was just an ordinary old man.

"Hello, sonny. Got some stuff there for the old grunters?"

Eric nodded, mutely, and held out his offering. What old grunters? What did he mean?

The Pig-man put down his bucket. He had ordinary hands, ordinary arms. He took the lid off. Eric held out the paper carrier, and the Pig-man's hand actually touched his own for a second. A flood of gratitude rose up inside him. The Pig-man tipped the scraps into the bucket and handed the carrier back.

"Thanks, sonny," he said.

"Who's it for?" Eric asked, with another rush of articulateness. His voice seemed to have a life of its own.

The Pig-man straightened up, puzzled. Then he laughed, in a gurgling sort of way, but not like a pig at all.

"Arh Aarh Harh Harh," the Pig-man went. "Not for me, if that's whatcher mean, arh harh."

He put the lid back on the bucket. "It's for the old grunters," he said. "The old porkers. Just what they likes. Only not fruit skins. I leaves a note, sometimes, about what not to put in. Never fruit skins. It gives 'em the belly-ache."

He was called the Pig-man because he had some pigs that he looked after.

"Thank you," said Eric. "Good night." He ran back towards the house, hearing the Pig-man, the ordinary old man, the ordinary usual normal old

41

man, say in his just ordinary old man's voice, "Good night, sonny."

So that was how you did it. You just went straight ahead, not worrying about this or that. Like getting into cold water. You just *did* it.

He slowed down as he got to the gate. For instance, if there was a question that you wanted to know the answer to, and you had always just felt you couldn't ask, the thing to do was to ask it. Just straight out, like going up to the Pig-man. Difficult things, troubles, questions, you just treated them like the Pig-man.

So that was it!

The warm light shone through the crack of the door. He opened it and went in. His mother was standing at the table, her hands still working the cake mixture about. She would let him scrape out the basin, and the spoon – he would ask for the spoon, too. But not straight away. There was a more important thing first.

He put the paper carrier down and went up to her. "Mum," he said. "Why can't Dad be with us even if Donald *is* here? I mean, why can't he live with us as well as Donald?"

His mother turned and went to the sink. She put the tap on and held her hands under it.

"Darling," she called.

"Yes?" came Donald's voice.

"D'you know what he's just said?"

"What?"

"He's just asked . . ." She turned the tap off and dried her hands, not looking at Eric. "He wants to know why we can't have Jack to live with us."

There was a silence, then Donald said, quietly, so that his voice only just reached Eric's ears, "That's a hard one."

"You can scrape out the basin," his mother said to Eric. She lifted him up and kissed him. Then she rubbed her cheek along his, leaving a wet smear. "Poor little Ekky," she said in a funny voice.

She put him down and he began to scrape out the pudding-basin, certain at least of one thing, that grown-ups were mad and silly and he hated them all, all, *all*.

Study Material

Abbreviations

adv.	adverb	*etc.*	and so on (Latin: *et cetera*)
A.E.	American English	*i.e.*	that is (Latin: *id est*)
B.E.	British English	*l./ll.*	line/lines
cf.	compare (Latin: *confer*)	*p./pp.*	page/pages
coll.	colloquial	*sl.*	slang
dial.	dialect(al)	*s.o.*	someone
e.g.	for example (Latin: *exempli gratia*)	*s.th.*	something
		usu.	usually
esp.	especially		

Pronunciation

Received Pronunciation (RP) as represented in Jones-Gimson, *English Pronouncing Dictionary* (EPD)

EPD 13th ed.

i	ship
ɔ	pot
u	put
ə:	bird
ei	make
əu	note
ai	bite
au	now
ɔi	boy
iə	here
ɛə	there
uə	poor

EPD 14th ed.

ɪ
ɒ
ʊ
ɜ:
eɪ
əʊ
aɪ
aʊ
ɔɪ
ɪə
eə
ʊə

Roald Dahl, Dip in the Pool

Biographical Notes

Roald Dahl (1916), British short story and screen writer, was born in South Wales, although his parents were Norwegians. After taking part in an expedition to explore the interior of Newfoundland, he worked for Shell in East Africa in the 1930s. When World War II broke out, he became a fighter pilot in the Royal Air Force (R.A.F.) and was severely wounded in the Lybian desert. In 1942, by now Assistant Air Attaché to the British Embassy in Washington, he began writing stories on his most exciting war experiences, first published in American magazines.

In 1945 these were reprinted in his first book, *Over to You* (including titles like *Yesterday Was Beautiful, Only This,* and *Someone Like You*). In 1953 his second book of short stories was published: *Someone Like You,* from which comes the humorous story *Dip in the Pool.* His best known book of stories is probably *Kiss Kiss* (1959) in which he shows a taste for slightly "sick" humour (e. g. *The Landlady,* which has macabre traits). Dahl has also written a number of screenplays, including the James Bond film *You Only Live Twice* (1967). He lives in Buckinghamshire and is married with four children.

I. 1. Vocabulary

6 dip	(coll.) a quick bathe
delicate ['delɪkɪt]	sensitive; easily made ill
to emerge from	to come out from, to appear
to creep (crept, crept)	to move slowly and quietly
to tuck rugs around	to wrap or put rugs (= woollen coverings) around (one's legs) to keep them warm
moderately rough ['mɒdərɪtlɪ 'rʌf]	rather rough (of weather/sea: stormy, violent, not calm)
genial (atmosphere) ['dʒiːnjəl]	cheerful, kind, friendly
complacent [kəm'pleɪsnt]	self-satisfied
air	general appearance
seasoned	*here:* having great experience
friction ['frɪkʃən]	the force which tries to stop one surface sliding over another
to roll	(of a ship) to swing from side to side with the movement of the waves

subtle ['sʌtl]	hardly noticeable
apprehension [,--'--]	fear, anxiety (esp. about the future)
unruffled	calm, not worried
smug	very pleased with oneself
to torture s.o.	to make s.o. feel great pain
she	the ship (which is grammatically feminine)
to brace oneself	*here:* to try to be seated firmly
purser	an officer who keeps a ship's accounts (Zahlmeister)
poached turbot	turbot (Steinbutt) cooked in gently boiling water
hollandaise ['hɒləndeɪz] sauce [sɔ:s]	
flutter	state of excited interest
to clutch	to hold tightly
7 There was just the **faintest suggestion of relish**	There was only the slightest sign of pleasure/enjoyment
to subside [səb'saɪd]	to get less
to thread one's way	to make one's way carefully
concealed [kən'si:ld]	hidden, intended not to be seen or known
remainder	rest
flock	*normally:* a flock of sheep; *here:* the passengers gathered round the purser
to take pride in	to be proud of
grave	serious (in manner)
anxious ['æŋkʃəs]	eager, having a strong wish to do s.th.
to make one's estimate ['estɪmɪt]	to calculate (*here:* the distance which the ship may cover within one day, i.e. "the day's run")
auction ['ɔkʃən]	*here:* a game of "selling numbers on the ship's daily run"
pool	money collected and gambled for
8 **to ponder s.th.**	to think s.th. over
to allow for	to take into consideration
intent (look) [ɪn'tent]	showing great attention
(half-)cocked	from to cock: to cause to stand up, e.g. The horse cocked its ears when it heard a noise. *Hence:* paying (great) attention, but not openly shown
straight from the horse's mouth	from a person who is at the source of information
range	the limits within which to place the bets (dependent on the captain's estimate)
to grab hold of	to catch hold of suddenly
rail	a fixed bar protecting people from falling
to well up	to rise like water in a well (Brunnen)

plumes of spray	suggesting a feather by their shape (spray: water in very small drops blown from the sea)
to slacken speed	to slow down
on account of	because of
9 dinner jacket	black jacket worn on formal occasions
auctioneer [ˌɔːkʃəˈnɪə]	the person leading an auction
desperate air [ˈdespərɪt]	with an impression of despair on his face
tremendous [trɪˈmendəs]	very great in amount, degree, consequence
to sell for	to be bought at (e.g. a newspaper selling for/at 10 p)
apiece	(adv.) each
currency [ʌ]	the money in use in a certain country
bills	(A.E.), B.E. banknotes (or: notes)
convertible	(of a car) having a roof that can be folded back
casual [ˈkæʒjʊəl]	careless, as if by chance
bid	offer of a price (at an auction sale)
10 to be knocked down for	to be sold for (cf. the auctioneer's hammer; phrase: to come under the hammer)
to fetch (a price)	to sell for, to bring in
panelling [ˈpænəlɪŋ]	woodwork covering a wall
to bid (bid, bid)	to offer to pay a certain price (esp. at an auction)
to figure	to calculate
Any advance on ...?	Is there anybody to make a higher bid?
to bid s.o. up	to make the price higher for s.o. by a further offer
bald [ɔː] (head)	having no hair (on his head)
beads of sweat [iː/e]	small drops of perspiration (Schweißtropfen)
11 Going ... Going ... Gone!	zum ersten, zum zweiten, zum dritten!
twenty-one hundred-odd pounds	a little more than 2,100 pounds (cf. 20-odd years)
charities	organizations helping the poor
gratifying	giving pleasure and satisfaction
gale	a very strong wind
to peer [ˈpɪə]	to look very carefully
porthole	a small round window in a ship
bunk	one of two beds fixed one above the other
to draw cheques	to write out cheques when you want to buy s.th.
instalments on s.th.	single (usu. monthly) payments which, in time, will complete full payment of s.th.
Encyclopaedia [enˌsaɪkləʊˈpiːdjə]	
there was no point in doing s.th.	it was useless/pointless to do s.th.
to put in reverse	to cause to move backward
astern [əˈstɜːn]	(adv.) of a ship: backward

12 Why **ever** not?	(adv.) giving emphasis to the question
afloat	floating on water
to knock 30 miles off the day's run	to cut, bring down the day's run by 30 miles
to taper	to become gradually narrower
bollard	a short, thick post where ships are fastened
to tread [e] (trod, trodden)	to walk, step
buttocks ['bʌtəks]	the part of the body on which one sits
advertent [əd'vɜ:tənt]	attentive, careful
to fail s.o.	to disappoint the hopes or trust of s.o.
to take a chance	to run a risk
13 **it occurs to me**	it comes into my mind
cinch	(sl.) s.th. done easily (Kleinigkeit)
lounge [laʊndʒ]	a comfortable sitting-room in a hotel, on a ship
apology [ə'pɒlədʒɪ]	a gesture (or statement) expressing regret for something you have done wrong
to edge away	to move away little by little
he retreated about ten paces	he walked back about ten steps
shark	fish, often dangerous to people (Hai)
to delay [dɪ'leɪ]	to stop for a time
to swing the balance in one's favour	*here:* to get a better chance of success
to haul [ɔ:] **up**	to pull up
lifeboat	small boat used for saving people
surreptitiously [ˌsʌrəp'tɪʃəslɪ]	(adv.) done secretly, esp. for dishonest reasons
14 **to assail**	to attack violently
to clear (the propeller)	to get far enough away from
belly flop	an awkward jump, landing on the belly
high dive	high platform in a swimming-pool
poised [pɔɪzd]	in a state of readiness to move
spreadeagled ['-'--]	with arms and legs spread out
lifebelt	a ring filled with cork
to swing (swung, swung)	to turn quickly (round)
(the ship's) wake	the track left by the ship in the water
tiny ['taɪnɪ]	very small indeed
foam	the whitish mass on the waves
bobbing	moving quickly and repeatedly up and down
speck	a small spot, dot
15 angular ['æŋɡjʊlə]	with bones clearly to be seen
to spot	to pick out with the eye, to see/recognize
spinster	an unmarried (old) woman
alert [ə'lɜ:t]	watchful, quick to see and act
to be meant to	to have to, to be supposed to (do s.th.)

2. Exercises

2.1. *Word-field study:*
Collect word material from the text of this story and group it under "Auction and money" and "Ship/sea and voyage". Do you know additional words and phrases?

2.2. *Grammar:*
Dahl sometimes uses the adjective form where Standard English would normally require an adverb. Try to find examples of this in the text.

II. Comprehension

1. What, at first sight, seems to be the theme of this story? — Refer to the literal meaning of its title.
2. Where is the story set and what do we learn about the weather?
3. Describe the general atmosphere on board the ship. — Is there a change in the passengers' mood?
4. At what point is Mr William Botibol introduced to the reader? — And what are the first things we get to know about him?
5. Who does he talk to for a considerable time?
6. Whispering urgently in the purser's ear, he asks quite a number of questions. Can you quote them in their correct order?
7. Why does Mr Botibol leave the dining-room for the open deck?
8. Can you describe Mr Botibol's looks and thoughts immediately before the beginning of the auction?
9. What sort of a game is the auction? — How does it work?
10. What has Mr Botibol decided to do? — What is his bid?
11. What is the weather like on the following morning? — Is that of any significance to his plans and intentions?
12. When in utter despair, he suddenly has an idea. What is it?
13. Mr Botibol is out on deck again. How is he dressed now and for what reason?
14. Why does he address the fat woman leaning over the rail?
15. How does the woman react when Mr Botibol jumps overboard?
16. Why does the lady not give the alarm? — Give reasons.
17. Are there any further implications in the title of the story?

Katherine Mansfield, The Doll's House

Biographical Notes

Katherine Mansfield was born in Wellington, New Zealand, in 1888. When she was 13 her father, a banker and industrialist, sent her to London, where she attended Queen's College. She returned to New Zealand in 1906, but, finding life there oppressively provincial, she gained permission to return to England two years later.

In the beginning her interests turned to music rather than to writing. In 1909 she married George Bowden, a musician, but left him after only a few days. In 1911 she met John Middleton Murry, who later became a famous literary critic. She obtained a divorce from Bowden in 1918 and subsequently married Murry.

Her brother's death in the First World War caused her to reconsider her New Zealand childhood. Her best stories are set in her native country. She won literary fame when *Bliss and Other Stories* was issued in 1920. Other collections of stories followed: *The Garden Party* (1922), *The Dove's Nest* (1923), *Something Childish* (1924) and *The Aloe* (1930). The latter three were published after her death from tuberculosis in Paris in 1923.

Her short stories depend less on outward event than on subtle description and analytical power. *The Doll's House* is strongly autobiographical: There was an Aunt Beryl, her mother's younger sister, and there were Mrs Kelvey and her daughters, who lived near Wellington.

I. 1. Vocabulary

16 carter	s.o. who drives a horse and cart
to prop up	to support, to keep in position
feed-room	room in which food for animals is kept
sacking	rough cloth for making sacks; *here:* coarse material used to wrap s.th. up
spinach ['spinidʒ]	vegetable whose green leaves are eaten (Spinat)
picked out with bright yellow	with bright yellow here and there to relieve the green
to gleam	to shine brightly
varnish	hard shining coating on the surface of s.th. (Überzug)
slab	a thick flat piece
streak	band, strip

porch	built-out roofed doorway (entrance) to a building
lump	mass of s.th. solid (usu. without a special shape; *but:* a lump of sugar)
congealed [kən'dʒi:ld]	thickened, having become stiff (always unpleasant)
to prise open	to force open
to peer	to look closely, as if unable to see well
mean	poor in appearance, shabby-looking
knocker	piece of metal on a door for knocking on it
17 cradle	small bed (boxed in or enclosed) for a baby, usu. made so that it can be moved
dresser	piece of kitchen furniture with open shelves above and cupboards below
jug	a pot with a handle and a lip for pouring liquids (e. g. a milk-jug)
amber ['æmbə]	yellowish-brown hard substance used for ornaments etc. (Bernstein)
globe	round glass used as a lampshade
to sprawl	to sit or lie with the arms and legs spread out loosely
to boast	to brag, to show off
bossy	fond of giving orders
to brush through	to touch when passing; *here:* to walk through, touching ...
buttercup	wild plant with yellow flowers (Butterblume, Hahnenfuß)
to traipse [treɪps]	to walk around aimlessly
tarred [ɑ:]	covered with tar (Teer)
palings	fence made of pointed pieces of wood
to jangle ['dʒæŋg(ə)l]	to make a hard unpleasant sound, as of metal striking against metal
to whip off	to take off quickly
to call the roll	to read the names (to check who is present and who is absent)
to beam	to smile happily
to flatter	to praise s.o. insincerely in order to please
18 **to nudge** [nʌdʒ]	to push slightly with the elbow
to giggle [gɪgl]	to laugh in a silly way
rude [ru:d]	impolite, wild
to shun	to avoid
spry	lively, active
gaolbird ['dʒeɪl-]	(sl.) person who is or has been in prison
conspicuous [kən'spɪkjʊəs]	attracting attention
stout	plump or fat

plain	ordinary, not pretty
freckles	spots on the face caused by sunburn
serge [sɜːdʒ]	strong cloth, usu. woven from wool
art-serge	artificial serge
perched	balanced precariously
to trim	to decorate or ornament
quill [kwɪl]	large tail feather
guy	person dressed in a queer-looking way
wish-bone	V-shaped bone in a chicken or bird, the ends of which can easily be pulled apart; *here:* a very lean person
to crop	to cut short
screwed up in her hand	twisted and held tightly in her hand
19 **tug**	sudden hard pull
twitch	sudden quick pull
to hover ['hɒvə]	*here:* to remain (wait) on the outskirts of a group, hopefully
to sneer	to smile in a mocking fashion that expresses proud dislike
shamefaced	timid; showing shame
teeny ['tiːnɪ]	tiny, very small
rage	strong but temporary interest; s.th. very fashionable
the dinner hour was given up to	the main theme discussed during the dinner hour was ...
johnny cake	cake made of maize (corn) flour
blob	spot of colour (suggestion of thickness)
the subject flagged	the interest ebbed away
20 in a very meaning way	indicating an important (hidden) thought, suggesting that she knows more than she is prepared to say
to snap	to flash (showing excitement)
squeal	a long, very high cry
to slide	to move your feet over a smooth surface without lifting them (as on ice)
to glide	to move along in a slow and graceful fashion
dragging one foot	pulling one foot behind
What a sell for Lena!	What a disappointment for Lena!
to titter	to give a silly, half-suppressed laugh (kichern)
to hiss	to make a nasty sibilant (s-sound) whisper through the teeth
spiteful	hateful, laughing at the misfortune of others
buggy	carriage pulled by one horse

	pinafore ['pɪnəfɔ:]	loose garment that doesn't cover the arms (and sometimes not the back), worn over a dress to keep it clean
	to thieve out (usu. to steal out)	to leave without anybody noticing
	dot	small spot
21	**to clamber**	to climb with some difficulty
	astounded	overcome (shocked) with surprise
	to gasp [ɑ:]	to catch the breath suddenly and in a way that can be heard
	to implore	to plead, to ask s.o. in a begging manner
	to frown	to draw the eyebrows together
	a stray cat	a cat without an owner, without a home
	to snort	to make a noise by blowing air violently out through the nose
	to undo	to loosen
	to give a start	to make a quick uncontrolled movement, as from sudden surprise and fear
22	to shoo	to drive away (usu. birds)
	to shrink together	to become smaller (because of shame, fear etc.)
	to huddle along	to hurry along with stooped shoulders
	dazed	bewildered
	they ... squeezed out of the white gate	they forced their way out through a small gap in the gate
	wicked ['wɪkɪd]	bad, immoral
	to slam (a door)	to shut (a door) violently and noisily
	to give a scolding	to blame with angry words
	ghastly	(coll.) terrible, unpleasant
	to hum	to sing with closed lips
	paddock	small, usu. enclosed, field of grass where horses are kept or exercised (Koppel); (Austral.) enclosed field
	creek	(B.E.) backwater, a long narrow body of water reaching from the sea, a lake etc. into the land; (A.E.) a small river
	wattle	Australian plant (acacia) with yellow flowers, chosen as an emblem of that country
	cross	(coll.) angry
	to stroke	to pass one's hand over gently (cats like being stroked)

2. Exercises

2.1 Put in the right preposition
1. Old Mrs Hay had been staying ... the Burnells.
2. The hook ... the side was stuck fast.
3. The children stood there gazing ... the little house.
4. There were pictures ... the walls.
5. The Burnell girls burned to boast ... their doll's house.
6. Lottie and Kezia knew the powers that went ... being eldest.
7. They were allowed to ask the girls ... school, two ... a time, to come and look.
8. ... the time they had reached the school the bell had begun to jangle.
9. Isabel tried to make ... for it by looking very important.
10. ... the playground and ... the road there was Lil marching in front and our Else holding ... to her.
11. Emmie nodded ... Isabel as she had seen her mother do ... those occasions.
12. The girls were deeply excited, wild ... joy.

2.2 Replace the word(s) in bold type
1. The father and mother dolls looked as **if** they had **become unconscious**.
2. The Burnell children wanted to **brag** about their new doll's house.
3. As the Burnells **determined what was fashionable** in all matters of behaviour, the Kelveys were **avoided** by everybody.
4. Our Else was always **holding on** to her sister's dress.
5. When Kezia mentioned the lamp nobody **cared**.
6. **Laughing in a silly way** Lena went over to the Kelveys.
7. Lena couldn't **stand** Lil's shamefaced smile.
8. The little Kelveys were **overcome with surprise**.
9. Our Else was looking at her sister with big **begging** eyes.
10. Pat **took off** the hook.

2.3 Adjective or adverb?
1. The smell of paint made Aunt Beryl feel (serious) ill.
2. There were two (solid) little chimneys glued on to the roof.
3. Who could (possible) mind the smell of such a (perfect) little house.
4. It was much more (exciting) than peering through the slit of a door.
5. What Kezia liked (frightful) was the lamp.

6. The children had to stand (quiet) in the courtyard.
7. Isabel tried to make up for it by looking very (mysterious).
8. They were the daughters of a (hard) working washerwoman.
9. Lil looked at Else very (doubtful). When they approached the doll's house she breathed (loud).
10. "Wicked, (disobedient) girl", said Aunt Beryl (bitter) to Kezia.

II. Comprehension

1. Why is the doll's house put into the courtyard and not into the house?
2. What is the difference between this doll's house and an ordinary one?
3. Why are the Burnell children and their friends so excited about the new house?
4. What does Kezia like best about the house?
5. Describe the relationship between the Burnell sisters and that between the two Kelvey sisters.
6. How does Isabel arouse the other girls' interest?
7. How do the majority of the girls behave when they crowd around Isabel to listen to her news?
8. Why do the Kelvey sisters not dare to approach the other girls?
9. What do Lil and "Our Else" look like?
10. Describe Lena's behaviour towards the Kelvey girls.
11. Why do the girls skip so high after Lena's spiteful action?
12. How does Kezia behave when the Kelvey girls turn up at the Burnells' house?
13. How does Aunt Beryl treat them when she sees them standing in front of the doll's house? What are the reasons for her behaviour?

Alun Lewis, The Lapse

Biographical Notes

Alun Lewis (1915—1944) grew up in a Welsh mining valley and witnessed the depression of the interwar years, though he himself enjoyed the relative security of a schoolmaster's home. The ugliness of industrialism, social and economic evils, and the warmth of his family life shaped his consciousness. He gained distinction as a history student at Manchester University, but research held no fascination for him. He joined the South Wales Borderers regiment and in 1942 was transferred to India. He was killed in an accident while on active service in Burma.

The Lapse is taken from *The Last Inspection* (1942), a collection of stories. Lewis's basic concern was with essentially simple people who somehow preserve their integrity and set personal loyalties against and above the impersonal forces around them. In one of his letters he wrote: "I find myself quite unable to express at once the passion of Love, the coldness of Death, and the fire that beats against resignation, acceptance. Acceptance seems so spiritless, protest so vain. In between the two I live."

I. 1. Vocabulary

23 **season ticket**	a ticket usable any number of times (as for railway or bus trips between two places) during a fixed period of time
to knit [nɪt]	to make clothes by using needles and wool
jumper	a kind of pullover
pork-pie hat	type of hat with a flat round top
to tuck s.th. against s.th. else	to push into a convenient position
shuttle	an instrument used in weaving (Schiffchen)
workwards	antonym: homewards
beat	rhythm
the Turk-Sib ['tɜːkˈsɪb]	the Turkistan-Siberian Railway
moujiks [ˈmuːʒɪks]	Russian peasants
to yawn [jɔːn]	to open the mouth wide, as when tired
slatternly	dirty, untidy
Bank holidays	public holidays in the British Isles, e.g. Easter Monday, Good Friday, Spring Holiday (the last Monday in May)
drab	cheerless, dull
hotchpotch	(usu. a number of things mixed up without any sensible order of arrangement); *here:* disorderly

backs	*here:* back gardens
to riddle the ashes	to pass the ashes through a sieve (so as to keep the rest of the coals)
to condemn s.o.	to state the punishment of a guilty person, esp. a punishment of death or long imprisonment
to serve	*here:* to spend a period of time in prison (e.g. to serve a sentence)
lifer	(sl.) *here:* a sentence of imprisonment for life
wrench [rentʃ]	a sudden pull
to swoop	to descend sharply
embankment	a raised structure along a river to hold back water or to carry a road or railway
to swirl [swɜ:l]	to move with twisting turns
drop	*here:* the height from the bridge to the river
sheer [ʃɪə]	straight down
pit of the stomach ['stʌmək]	the hollow place just below the bones of the chest (thought of as being the place where fear is felt)
to flash	to move very fast (like lightning)
accelerando [ækˌseləˈrændəʊ]	(Ital.) moving faster
cutting	a passage cut through land or a forest so that a road, railway, etc. can pass
to go to the pictures	to go to the cinema
nap	(familiar) a short sleep, esp. during the day
stroll	a walk for pleasure
grand	splendid, important, great
to wolf s.th. (down)	to eat quickly (with greed), like a wolf
to sweat [swet]	(schwitzen)
satchel	a school-bag carried over the shoulders
scrimpy	= skimpy: meagre, thin
to poke	to push sharply out of or through an opening
fringe	*here:* (Ponyfrisur)
prominent	standing or stretching out (beyond a surface)
semi-detached ['semɪ] **houses**	joined to another house on one side only
huddle	a number of things, close together and not in ordered arrangement
to snooze	(informal) to have a short sleep (cf. 'nap')
oak-apple	a small round brown growth that forms on the leaves of oak trees round the eggs laid by an insect (Gallapfel)
lap	the front part of a seated person between the waist and the knees
to daunt [dɔ:nt]	to cause to lose courage or the will to act
to smash	to destroy by causing to break into pieces

communication cord [kɔ:d]	emergency brake
to batter at	beat hard and repeatedly
shudder	an uncontrollable shake
biscuit facade [ˈbɪskɪt fəˈsɑ:d]	brownish front of building
to fumble	to move the fingers or hands awkwardly and nervously in an attempt to do s.th.
to tug at s.th.	to pull s.th. with force or much effort
25 footplate	platform in a locomotive for the driver and fireman
hoot	the sound made by a car horn, foghorn or by a steam-whistle
to scramble	to move or climb quickly
to blaspheme [-ˈfi:m]	to use bad language, curse
to quiver	to tremble (a little)
to slouch	to walk in a tired way
to slump	to fall/drop heavily
to clench	to press firmly together
smuts	bits of dirt or soot
shriek	scream; *here:* the sound made by a steam-whistle
to tidy s.th.	to make s.th. neat, put s.th. in order again
to skewer [ˈskju:ə]	to fasten with a long wooden or metal pin
to slink (slunk, slunk) **past s.th.**	to move quietly and secretly, move in a guilty manner as though ashamed

2. Exercises

2.1 Word-field study:
Make a list of all the words in the story that have to do with the railway.
Make a list of all the words that denote movement. Find paraphrases and/or German equivalents.
Make a list of all the adjectives that have negative connotations.

2.2 Phrasal expressions:
Learn the following expressions; familiarize yourself with the meanings they have in the text and then make up sentences of your own.
He was waiting for the train to start — these last five years — twice a day/five times a week — to be condemned to serve a sentence — I don't know what to do/where to go/who to ask, etc. — I can't make up my mind — she'll be sitting opposite me — her shoes need soling/the walls need papering — to feel sorry for a person — all of a sudden — in astonishment

2.3 Fill in the gaps:

Refer to the vocabulary lists, the word-fields and the phrasal expressions above.

1. Henry showed his . . . to the porter.
2. He had done this journey many times . . . .
3. Not many of them knew that they had been . . . a lifer.
4. I don't know what . . ., I can never make . . . .
5. She'll be sitting . . . Henry.
6. Perhaps she lived in the . . . houses on the right?
7. The woman's shoes . . . soling.
8. Something made him want to . . . the windows, pull . . . and scream.
9. Somehow he . . . for her.
10. And then, . . ., Henry got up and walked down the car.
11. He fumbled and . . . the carriage door.
12. To move rapidly, turning all the time =
13. To walk in an awkward careless manner =
14. To drop heavily =
15. To move in a guilty way =

II. Comprehension

A. 1. How does the story begin and what does Henry do?
   2. Which route does the train take?
   3. What happens at "halt number one"?
   4. What does Henry do when the train stops "with a shudder"?
   5. Is Henry on the train when it starts moving again?
   6. Write a summary of Henry's actions.
B. 1. How long and how often has Henry done this journey?
   2. What does Henry think about while the train is passing the outskirts of the town and reaches the open country?
   3. What details do we learn about the girl?
   4. Why does Henry want to pull the communication cord?
   5. How does he feel when he gets back on the train?
   6. Write a summary of Henry's thoughts.

James Joyce, Eveline

Biographical Notes

James Joyce was born in Dublin in 1882. He was the eldest of "sixteen or seventeen children", as his father put it.

He was educated at Jesuit schools and later attended the Catholic University College, Dublin, where he studied Latin, Italian, French and even Norwegian so that he could read Ibsen's plays. Despite his Catholic upbringing Joyce turned away from Catholicism.

In 1904 he married Nora Barnacle. Unable to make a living as a writer, he left Ireland in 1904 to work abroad as a language teacher. Also in 1904 he began writing *Dubliners* (a group of short stories from which *Eveline* is taken), which he completed the following year; but it was not until 1914 that he could find a publisher for his book. In *Dubliners* Joyce set out to "write a chapter of the moral history of my country ... under four of its aspects: childhood, adolescence, maturity and public life."

His largely autobiographical novel *A Portrait of the Artist as a Young Man* was published in 1916. In 1921 he finished *Ulysses,* which made him a great innovator of modern literature.

James Joyce suffered many hardships, living in poverty for most of his life and enduring several eye operations. He died in Zurich in 1941.

In *Eveline* he describes an Irish girl lacking the strength of faith, hope and love, so that although she longs to go away she remains at home.

I. 1. Vocabulary

26 Eveline ['evlın/'i:vlın]

nostril	either of the two openings in the nose
odour ['əʊdə]	smell, esp. an unpleasant one
cretonne ['kretɒn]	heavy cotton cloth with printed patterns (designs) on it, used for curtains etc.
to clack	to make one or more sudden quick sharp sounds as of two pieces of wood struck together
to crunch	to make a crushing noise as of eating nuts, walking on frozen snow etc.
cinder ['sındə]	coal which looks like stone after it has been burnt
Keogh [kjəʊ]	
blackthorn	thorny shrub (bush) which has white blossoms and purple fruit (Schlehdorn)
to keep nix	to be on the look-out

Blessed ['blesɪd] ...	der/die Selige ...
Margaret Mary Alacoque	French nun who had a vision
a casual word	a word in passing
to consent to	to agree to
shelter	protection; a place to live in
27 stores	a shop in which many different types of goods are sold
to have an edge on s.o.	*Irish usage:* to have a hostile attitude towards s.o.
palpitation	beating of the heart that is irregular or too fast
to go for s.o.	to beat (attack) s.o.
latterly	recently, of late
invariable	constant; *here:* inevitable
squabble ['skwɒbl]	quarrel, esp. over s.th. unimportant
to weary [ɪə]	to make tired
to squander [ɒ]	to spend foolishly or wastefully
to leave to the charge of s.o.	to leave for s.o. to look after
Buenos Ayres ['bwenəs'aɪərɪz]	modern spelling: Buenos Aires
28 a peaked cap	a cap with a curved part which sticks out in front above the eyes
to tumble	to fall disorderly
The Bohemian Girl [bəʊ'hi:mjən]	opera by M. W. Balfe, an Irish composer
elated	filled with joy
to be courting	to try to win the love of s.o. with the aim of marrying
lass [æ]	a young man's girlfriend
Straits of Magellan [mə'gelən]	a narrow passage of water between the South American continent and Tierra del Fuego
Patagonian	inhabitant of Patagonia (southern part of Argentina)
chap	(coll.) fellow, man, boy
to be laid up	to be kept indoors or in bed with an illness
Howth [həʊθ]	place near Dublin
bonnet ['bɒnɪt]	sort of hat tied under the chin
air	tune, melody
close [kləʊs]	lacking fresh air, warm and stuffy
29 **to strut**	to walk in a proud way, trying to look important
to muse [mju:z]	to allow one's thoughts to wander
spell	charm, magical power
quick	the most sensitive part, depth of being
commonplace [ɒ]	ordinary
commonplace sacrifices ['sækrɪfaɪsɪz]	the constant little sacrifices (Opfer) that entirely made up her everyday life

Derevaun Seraun ['derəvɔːnsə'rɔːn]	*corrupt Gaelic possibly meaning:* "in the end only worms"
to fold s.o. in one's arms	to wrap one's arms around s.o.
to sway	to swing (move) from side to side
to catch a glimpse of	to have a quick, incomplete view of
quay [kiː]	landing-place where ships can be (un)loaded
porthole	small (usu. round) window in a ship
maze	*here:* confusion, unhappiness
distress	pain and sorrow
mournful	sad
nausea ['nɔːzjə]	a feeling of sickness
fervent ['fɜːvənt]	passionate, intense
to clang	to make a loud ringing sound
to clutch	to hold tightly
frenzy ['frenzɪ]	a state of wild uncontrolled feeling
anguish ['æŋgwɪʃ]	extreme pain, esp. of the mind

2. Exercises

2.1 Put in the right preposition
1. A yellowing photograph hung ... the wall.
2. She would not cry many tears ... leaving the Stores.
3. She hated the squabbling for money ... Saturday nights.
4. Frank had started as a deck boy ... a pound a month ... a ship.
5. One day they had all gone ... a picnic to the Hill of Howth.
6. She remembered her father putting ... her mother's bonnet.
7. The street organ reminded her ... the promise ... her mother.
8. She stood ... the swaying crowd in the station.
9. If she went she would be ... the sea with Frank the following day.
10. He was shouted ... to go on, but he still called ... her.

2.2 Replace the word(s) in bold type
1. She had **agreed** to going away with him.
2. Two children had been left **for her to look after**.
3. Her mother had led a life of **everyday** sacrifices.
4. Through the white doors she caught **sight of** the black boat.
5. The boat blew a long **sad** whistle into the mist.
6. A feeling of **sickness** awoke within her.
7. Her hands **tightly held on to** the iron bar.

II. Comprehension

1. Give a short summary of Eveline's youth. What does she particularly remember?
2. Why does Eveline believe that she won't cry many tears when she goes away?
3. What role has she played in the house since her mother's death?
4. What are her feelings when she goes out with Frank to the theatre?
5. What promise had she given to her mother?
6. What kind of life had her mother led?
7. What does Eveline expect Frank to give her?
8. Describe her feelings when she is about to leave for Buenos Aires.

Alan Sillitoe, On Saturday Afternoon

Biographical Notes

Alan Sillitoe (born 1928), was the second of five children born into a Nottingham working-class family. His childhood coincided with the great economic depression which made his father jobless until 1939. The experience of living in poverty made a deep impression upon his mind and was reflected later in his writing. His main theme was to be working-class life in industrial Nottingham.

At the age of 14 Sillitoe left school to work in the Raleigh Bicycle Factory, where his father was also employed. From 1947 to 1948 he served with the R.A.F. (Royal Air Force) in Malaya and trained as a radio operator. While in hospital for a year with tuberculosis, he began writing poems, stories and a novel, all of which he destroyed.

At last, in 1958, his career as a writer began with the publication of his first novel, *Saturday Night and Sunday Morning*, which is still his most highly praised work of fiction. In the following year *The Loneliness of the Long-Distance Runner* appeared — his first volume of short stories, which includes *On Saturday Afternoon*. The film versions of these books helped to make him known to a wider public as a promising young writer speaking with the authority and language of an insider and avoiding the "heroization and sentimentalization" of his working-class protagonists.

I. 1. Vocabulary

Alan Sillitoe makes use of quite a number of dialect speech forms in his stories. The following list of "corrupt forms" will help you to understand the text better.

ain't	hasn't, isn't	messen [mɪˈsen]	myself
summat	something	'issen	himself
yo'/yer	you	'un	one
yer	your	wain't	won't
ye're	you're, you are	ter	to
wi'	with	gi'	give
o'	of	he'd broke	he'd broken
'ang	hang	tek	take
'e	he	don't	doesn't
ter 'ang	to hang		

30	**bloke**	(sl.) fellow, chap
	black	in a bad mood
	to be fed up	(coll.) to be unhappy, discontented, tired
	to go to the pictures	to go to the cinema
	'course	(short for) of course
	to string oneself up	to hang oneself
	kid	(coll.) a young child
	(the) old man	(low coll.) one's father
	fag	(sl.) cigarette
	saccharine ['sækəri:n]	a substitute for normal sugar
	to back out	(coll.) to retreat (from difficulty); *here:* to leave the house
	to come for s.o.	to attack s.o.
	oil-stained	having dark spots of oil
	Sunday-joint	*here:* having the size or look of a Sunday joint (a big piece of meat, eaten on Sundays: Sonntagsbraten)
	maulers [ɔ:]	(sl.) hands
	scrunched forward	bent forward
	to clear out	(coll.) to leave, often quickly
	mam	(coll.) mother
	to be in	to be in the house/at home
	(she says) sharp	*here for:* sharply (adverb)
	bleddy (usu. bloody)	(sl.) swear word used in angry speech or to give force to a value judgement
	to tip up	to cause to fall over, to knock over
	to hunch	to pull one's back into a rounded shape (cf. hunchback: a misshapen back)
	broody	having or showing sadness and silence (as with self-pity or unhappy thoughts)
	to go crackers	(sl.) to go mad, crazy, insane
	to sling (slung, slung)	to throw violently
	to mash (some tea)	(dial.) to make tea
	black (looks)	sad, dismal, gloomy, threatening (looks)
	It stands to reason	It is obvious; it is clear
	to carry on	to behave in a strange manner
31	clink	(sl.) prison
	plugged	*here:* not having the energy to leave
	bookie	(coll.) a bookmaker (he takes bets on horses, dogs, etc.)
	What's up wi' yo'?	(dial.) What's the matter with you?
	I feel badly	*here for:* bad (adj.)
	to fib	(coll.) to tell an unimportant lie

a fit (of anger)	*here:* a sudden and transitory state of anger (Anfall)
double-quick	more than quick
what with	(adv.) used for introducing the causes of s.th. (bad)
to bash away	to make an uninterrupted, loud noise by striking or knocking heavily
yard-end	the far end of the (partly) enclosed area next to or behind the house
parson ['pɑːsn]	Church of England priest
to droop [uː]	to hang/bend downwards
square meal	proper, substantial meal
nosy	(derogative & informal) interested in things that do not concern one
to gossip	to talk about other people's private affairs
to trudge [ʌ]	to walk heavily, wearily
pawnshop ['pɔːnʃɒp]	the place where you leave (valuable) things to borrow money (cf. to go to the pawnbroker's)
mate	friend, fellow (used as a form of address, esp. among working-class men)
to cackle	to laugh
she cackled on the other side of her fat face	she did not laugh at all
coil (of rope)	piece of rope twisted into a circular shape
32 **downtown**	(esp. A. E.) the centre of a town or city (cf. uptown: the residential areas)
bogger (usu. bugger)	(low coll.) fellow, chap; often a foolish, annoying person (also a taboo word: a sodomite, homosexual)
light-fitting	wire hanging down from the ceiling and to which a lamp can be fastened
it did him for what he wanted	it served his purpose
serial ['sɪərɪəl]	a story appearing in parts, often at fixed times (e.g. on TV), a series of films/programmes
nettled	(coll. & dial.) peevish, ill-/bad-tempered
to scram	(sl.) to clear out
fancy	not ordinary (adj. used attributively only)
gob	(sl.) mouth
dresser	piece of kitchen furniture with open shelves above and cupboards below
33 **pally** [æ]	(coll.) friendly (cf. pal)
bits and bobs	(coll.) bits and pieces, odds and ends
coppers	(coll.) for halfpennies and/or pennies (old currency before 1971 only)

missus	(dial. & low coll.) wife
to swear (swore, sworn)	to state firmly (cf. to swear an oath on the Bible)
worse luck	cf. bad luck (Pech); *here:* unluckier still
clock	(sl.) face
to back	to move backwards
to fly	to flee
to lead s.o. a dog's life	to cause s.o. to have a miserable life
to swing (swung, swung)	*here:* to shake
popping (eyes)	staring (eyes), almost springing/popping out of someone's head
goz	(sl.) look
pal [æ]	(coll.) close friend
so's I could have my cake and eat it	so that I could have a double advantage
tit for tat	(informal) s.th. (normally unpleasant) in return for s.th. else
butt-end	end of cigarette
firegrate, fireback	parts of the fireplace (Feuerrost; Brandmauer)
34 to wriggle ['rɪgl]	to move/twist from side to side
I took a runner	*here:* I rushed forward (like a centre-forward in the football team of Nottingham Forest)
scooting	(coll.) moving quickly & suddenly
muffler	(esp. old use) a sort of scarf
to chafe	to rub; to press, strike against
scarecrow ['skeəkrəʊ]	a human-like object (often of old clothes upon sticks) set up in the fields to keep birds away from the crops
to flap	to move violently up and down
dose [dəʊs]	a measured amount (esp. of liquid medicine)
salts	short for: Epsom salt(s), magnesium sulphate, used as medicine
bulb	the glass part of an electric lamp that gives the light
dizzy	feeling as if everything were turning round
thump	a dull, heavy sound
colic	severe pains in the belly
tut-tutting	making noises of disapproval
the balls-up	(sl.) mess (cf. to make a mess of; to spoil)
hinge [hɪndʒ]	metal part around which a door or gate swings
copper (also: **cop**)	(sl. & coll.) policeman
to head for	to move towards, to go to
to stride (strode, stridden)	to walk with long steps
to nark	(sl.) to inform the police

to tip s.o. off	(coll.) to give a hint to s.o.
happen	(dial., North of England) perhaps
to catch on	(sl.) to understand, to grasp the meaning of
to slit	to make a long cut
peepers	(sl.) eyes
approved school	school for young criminals/delinquents
to pinch	(sl.) to steal
lead piping [led]	tubes of lead (Bleirohre)
35 **to croak**	to make a noise like a frog or a raven
nay	(dial.) no
though [ðəʊ]	however, but; in spite of the fact; nevertheless (never at the beginning of a clause!)
to let on	(coll.) to tell a secret (usu. in the negative form)
to be in for it	(coll.) to be in trouble, due to receive punishment
six-months cold	(sl.) a period of six months in prison
to dish out	(coll.) to serve
grub	(sl.) food
to spill s.th. to s.o.	(sl.) to tell s.o. s.th.
daft [ɑː]	silly, stupid, mad
to cease [siːs]	to end
to chuck	(sl.) to throw
he went off for a pee	(coll.) he went to the lavatory
Not much 'e ain't.	(sl.) of course he is. (Und ob er das ist.)
36 to heave	(coll.) to lift and throw
ward [ɑː]	a room in a hospital containing a certain number of beds
to finish s.o. off	(low coll.) to kill s.o.
the black coal-bag locked inside you	image for the 'condition of blackness which finds no way out'
to sling oneself	(sl.) to throw oneself
sardine-tin [ˈsɑːdiːnˈtɪn]	(Sardinendose)
rotten	(sl.) bad, nasty, worthless
your rotten sack-bag of a body	your worthless body
to do oneself in	(sl.) to kill oneself
half-barmy	(sl.) half-mad
to scream (usu. cry) blue murder	to utter loud cries of terror or alarm

2. Exercises

2.1 Re-phrase in more formal language
1. He ain't got no fags.
2. What's that rope for, mate? — It's to 'ang messen wi'.
3. It wain't hold up, mate.
4. Yer wain't forget to kick that chair away?
5. I'd never 'ave thought it. I thought he'd got that daft idea out of his head.

2.2 Consult your dictionary and re-word avoiding slang expressions
1. He walked by me puffing a fag.
2. He made ever such a fancy knot with that rope, as though he'd been a sailor or summat.
3. He wasn't looking black at all, nowhere near as black as anybody in our family.
4. It was marvellous though, the way the brainless bastards had put him in a ward.
5. I didn't like the copper, because he'd got a couple of my mates sent to approved school.

II. Comprehension

1. Who is the narrator of this story? — Give precise details.
2. What is its main subject?
3. Where does the action take place?
4. What are we told about the narrator's family, especially his father and himself? Summarize.
5. Give an outline of what happens inside the man's house.
6. Describe the man who tries to commit suicide.
7. Why is the narrator so disappointed when he leaves the man's house?
8. Why does the "copper" arrest the man?
9. What happens to the man in the end?
10. What are the conclusions the boy draws from his tale of despair? Sum up the main results of his learning process.
11. What is the apparent theme of the story? — What is it really concerned with?
12. Does the title *On Saturday Afternoon* have any relevance to the actual story?
13. Think of other titles for this story. Explain their significance.

John Wain, A Message from the Pig-Man

Biographical Notes

John Barrington Wain, English novelist, poet, short story writer, and critic was born in Stoke-on-Trent, Staffordshire, in 1925. His father, a successful dentist, was the first of his family to emerge from the working class. John Wain writes of himself: "I was the average provincial schoolboy with no intellectual interests. My school work, which was in any case disorganized by the war, lagged sadly, and when on leaving school I expressed a wish to go to the university, I was not considered intelligent enough even to attempt a scholarship examination. I simply walked out of school and walked into Oxford, where, at that time, even backward youths like myself could get in easily if they could pay the fees. I obtained the First Class degree, from which I infer that Oxford had managed to cure my backwardness to some extent."

In 1973 he was elected Professor of Poetry at Oxford University. He enjoys skiing, canoeing, walks and nature study. He is an accomplished and prolific critic and literary journalist. He does much lecturing, editing, film and drama reviewing, radio and television work. With regard to his work he says: "I treat each work as a new beginning; I think the writer's task is to perceive as much as he can of the truth about human life and to pass on that truth to the reader, without distortion or falsification, by whatever means he can command."

Among his principal works are: *Hurry on Down*, 1953 (novel); *Nuncle and Other Stories*, 1960 (from which *A Message from the Pig-Man* is taken); *Preliminary Essays*, 1957.

I. 1. Vocabulary

37 **alteration** [ɔ:]	change
pointless	meaningless
it wants a lot of looking after	it needs a lot of attention
spare room	a room kept for visitors and guests
something to go on	*here:* signs, hints
to fit s.th. up	to arrange s.th. so that it works
rolling-stock	everything on wheels that belongs to a railway, except locomotives
to pull a face	*here:* to make a show of regret
38 **to hold on to s.o.**	to cling to, or embrace, s.o.

to live up to s.th.	to keep a high standard that is demanded by s.th.
to dart (in, along)	to move suddenly and quickly
not . . ., anyway	(jedenfalls nicht)
to ram s.th. into s.o.	to tell s.o. s.th. again and again so as to make him learn it
to look both ways	to look left and right before crossing the road
stuff [ʌ]	*here:* nonsense, rubbish
notice	"beneath the notice of" = of no importance to
spine	the row of bones in the centre of the back
to tingle	to feel a slight prickly sensation (of cold or fear)
peelings	skin removed from a fruit, vegetable, etc.; *here:* from potatoes
damp	rather wet
lid	the cover of a pot, box, etc.
39 snout	the nose and mouth of a pig
trotter	a pig's foot
sober [əʊ]	serious, without emotion
to imply	*here:* to mean
to duck s.o. into sleep	*here:* (in den Schlaf versenken)
swing	a seat held by ropes and on which one can move backwards and forwards
to crowd out	to extinguish, to push out of one's mind
to clatter (about)	to make a rattling sound (e.g. pots and pans and dishes clattered on the shelf)
in anticipation	full of expectation
to haul [ɔ:]	to pull (hard)
tremendously [-'-]	extremely
40 to scrape out	remove what is left in the basin with a spoon and then lick it
(paper) **carrier** ['kærɪə]	strong paper bag (for carrying goods away from a shop)
scraps	pieces of food left over after a meal
joyous	full of joy
to frown	draw the brows together in anger, so as to show disapproval
to nip along	(informal) to hurry
technique [tek'ni:k]	
41 dusk	the time when daylight is fading
to lurch [lɜ:tʃ]	to move with irregular sudden movements
gait [eɪ]	a way of walking
hunched (shoulders)	(shoulders) pulled into a rounded shape
to crush	to press tightly
pail	bucket

to plod [ɒ]	to walk slowly esp. with heavy steps; *here:* imitating the sound of "plodding footsteps" on the road
ruse [ruːz]	trick (to deceive an opponent)
to pounce [paʊns]	to move suddenly in order to seize s.th. or s.o., esp. for food
wicked ['wɪkɪd]	evil
rasping squeak [ɑː] [iː]	(krächzendes Quieken)
to jog	to move slowly and unsteadily; to move up and down
raging ['reɪdʒɪŋ]	violent, intense
tide	*here:* an upward movement like that of the sea
grunter	(coll.) pig (imitating the sound pigs make)
mutely ['mjuːtlɪ]	saying nothing
flood [ʌ] **of gratitude**	a sudden feeling of thankfulness
to tip (s.th. into s.th. else)	to pour (a substance) from one container into another
articulateness [ɑːˈtɪkjʊlɪtnɪs]	ability to express one's ideas clearly
to straighten up [eɪ]	to get up from a bent-over position
whatcher	(coll.) = what you
porker	young pig, specially fattened for food
belly-ache [eɪk]	pain in the stomach
42 sink	a large basin in the kitchen, for washing pots, vegetables, etc., fixed to a wall
That's a hard one	(coll.) That's a difficult question to answer
smear [ɪə]	spot made by some sticky, wet material (like tears)

2. Exercises

2.1 Phrasal verbs:

Consult your dictionary and learn the following list of phrasal verbs (verb + preposition/adverb); if you are in doubt as to the exact meaning of a verb, find the German equivalent.

to bring s.th. about — to get off — to go on — to go straight ahead — to look after — to look like — to hold on to s.th./s.o. — to live up to s.th. — to turn out to be — to come to — to think of s.th. — to catch s.o. up — to drag s.o. off — to take s.th. off — to slow down — to live with s.o. — to turn s.th. off (e.g. a tap, the TV, the radio)

2.2 Word-fields:

— Collect all the words that characterize the Pig-man.
— Collect all verbs of motion and paraphrase their meanings or look up their German equivalents.

2.3 Phrasal expressions:

Learn the following list of collocations; if you don't understand or know their meanings in English, consult your dictionary for the German equivalents.

to feel all right about s.th. — he did not mind sharing his room — in fact — to do s.th. in a mad/silly/funny way — he taught/showed him how to (fit s.th. together) — I can't do anything about it — it seems likely — all the same — it was his own fault — this seemed strange/this looks funny/she felt soft/to go cold — to be sorry for s.o. — what does he look like? — what difference is there between ... and ... — all the better — it takes some time (to count ten) — he's gone — out of the way — to seize s.o. by the hand

2.4 Fill in the gaps:

Refer to the vocabulary lists and the phrasal verbs and expressions above.
1. Being called 'Eric' was just one of those changes, not a disturbing ... .
2. The spare room was ... always empty.
3. Eric ... all right ... Donald's being in the house.
4. Eric wouldn't have ... sharing his bedroom with a baby.
5. His mother ... to Donald all the time.
6. Probably it was his ... that everything seemed strange.
7. He was not ... to his flannel trousers.
8. The Pig-man was nothing to be afraid of; he probably just ... funny.
9. Instead ... him, he went outside to see him.
10. If he walked on all fours, ... would there be between him and a pig?
11. Then his mother kissed him, ... nice; she ... soft.
12. When he went down to the swings he was far from ... the Pig-man.
13. Eric went into the kitchen and took the brown-paper ... full of peelings and ... .
14. "If you nip along, dear, you can easily ... ."
15. He might ... quickly when his wicked little eyes saw a tasty little boy.
16. He was called the Pig-man, because he had some pigs that he ... .
17. So that was how you did it. You just went ... .
18. She went to the ... , put the tap on and held her hands ... it. Then she ... the tap ... .

2.5 Analyze the following structures with the help of your grammar:
1. he felt all right about his being in the house (p. 37, l. 8)
2. he wouldn't have minded + ing (p. 37, ll. 11—12)

3. when they did give you s.th./Do be a sweet boy/I do believe I heard him (p. 37, ll. 22—23; p. 39, l. 36; p. 40, ll. 23—24)
4. seem/look strange/go cold/feel soft (p. 38, ll. 6, 12, 27; p. 39, l. 17)
5. Did they want him to meet the Pig-man? (p. 40, l. 10)
6. he would have little eyes (p. 39, ll. 1—2)

II. Comprehension

1. What does the reader learn about Eric from the beginning of the story?
2. What is Eric's relationship to the other characters of the story?
3. What problem is Eric confronted with at the beginning?
4. What does he think about himself?
5. How does he feel about the Pig-man?
6. What shape does the Pig-man take on in the boy's imagination "before it came to a crisis"?
7. Describe the atmosphere up to the moment Eric is asked to go out to the Pig-man.
8. Describe what the boy thinks and feels when his mother sends him out.
9. What are his feelings when he meets the Pig-man?
10. How does he feel about the Pig-man on his way home?
11. What does the phrase 'to treat (problems) like the Pig-man' mean to Eric?
12. What does Eric do after his encounter with the Pig-man?
13. What is his mother's reaction?

Now write a **summary** of the story using your answers to the comprehension questions as a guide.

Glossary of Literary Terms

Acting time: The time covered by the action of a narrative. E.g. the acting time in *Dip in the Pool* is one evening and part of one morning. (Cf. *Narrating time, Compression* and *Expansion*).

Action: The action of a story is a series of events usually arranged so as to have three recognizable parts: the beginning *(introduction/exposition)*, the middle *(rising action, complication; crisis, climax, turning-point; falling action)* and the end *(dénouement, catastrophe, resolution)*.

In contrast to real life, action in fiction is an ordered whole which "imitates in words a sequence of human activities, with a power to affect our opinions and emotions in a certain way". It is the basic principle in all fiction and arouses the reader's interest: it makes him eager to learn what is going to happen and/or how the problems faced by the characters are going to be solved. Action produces tension, suspense or surprise. (Cf. R. S. Crane, *The Concept of Plot*, p. 142).

Anticlimax: A stylistic effect resulting from a sudden drop of interest or importance.

Atmosphere: Mood or feeling partly created by the description of events, places and situations in a story and partly by the author's style. The various elements that constitute a piece of fiction, such as *setting, characterization, theme*, etc. also contribute to its atmosphere.

Author: see *Point of view*.

Catastrophe: The change which brings about the final event in a play or narrative. (Cf. *Dénouement*).

Character — flat, round: Characters are the "persons" in a narrative work, whose qualities are expressed in what they say and what they do. A flat character is "constructed round a single idea or quality" and is presented in outline without much individualizing detail, and so can be fairly adequately described in a single phrase or sentence.

A round character is complex in temperament and motivation and is represented with subtle particularity. (Cf. E. M. Forster, *Aspects of the Novel*).

Characterization: There are several different ways of presenting a character in fiction.

Explicit presentation: Here the omniscient narrator describes the outward appearance and the psychological and moral nature of a character. The telling of the story from the viewpoint of one or several characters whose thoughts and feelings are revealed in the process also serves to characterize those persons (cf. *Point of view, Selective omniscience*).

***Implicit* presentation:** A character is presented in terms of his or her environment. If a person lives in strange surroundings he is assumed to be strange himself. Since the narrator does not tell us explicitly, the reader is expected to draw his own conclusions.

Presentation *through action:* The narrator refrains from giving direct comments. Character is revealed through action.

Chiasmus: The crosswise arrangement of contrasted terms, the second of two syntactically parallel phrases reversing the order of the first.
Example: Too old to live, to die too young.

Climax: The highest point of reader interest, the moment of the highest *tension*.

Comic relief: A humorous episode in a serious or tragic context, designed to alleviate tension, add variety, counterpoint and enhance the tragic significance.

Complication: The device of bringing the conflicting forces together.

Compression: *Narrating time* is shorter than *acting time*, i.e. the action narrated took longer than it takes to tell the story. The narrator picks out events that seem important to him and omits or summarizes events and actions that do not. (Cf. *Expansion*).

Crisis: The highest point of the *complication* in the action, when forces and counterforces have met and the direction which the action must now take is determined (cf. *Turning-point*). In strict terminology, crisis refers only to structural and plot elements, whereas *climax* refers to the highest point of reader/audience interest.

Dénouement: The final *resolution* or untying of the plot. (Cf. *Catastrophe*).

Digression: The introduction of material which is either unrelated or only indirectly or distantly related to the main subject of a piece of writing.

Episode: A single incident presented as one continuous action, having a unity within itself. It is usually accompanied by other episodes so as to create a larger unit.

Expansion: *Narrating time* is longer than *acting time*. This may happen if the outward action is short and the omniscient narrator describes a person's thoughts and feelings. (Cf. *Compression*).

Exposition, Introduction: Terms used in discussing the structure of a narrative or play to denote that portion in which the author sets forth the information needed by the reader in order to understand the *plot* and the situation. It creates the *tone* (the author's attitude), establishes the *setting*, introduces the main *characters* and supplies other facts necessary for an understanding of the plot.

External action: The sequence of outward, observable events. (Cf. *Internal action*).

Extrinsic approach: A method of interpretation which is based on or includes material outside the literary work, e.g. the author's biography, sociological findings, etc. (Cf. *Intrinsic approach*).

Falling action: The action following the *crisis*, because it is thought of as descending from the highest point towards the *dénouement*. This action is the logical outcome of the conflicting forces that combined in the rising action to reach the *turning-point*. (Cf. *Action*).

"I" as protagonist/"I" as witness: see *Point of view.*

Interior monologue: see *Stream of consciousness.*

Internal action: The action that goes on inside the protagonist's or another character's mind; the learning process or development that he undergoes. (Cf. *External action*).

Intrinsic approach: A method of interpretation which relies solely on the text itself and which does not admit external evidence. (Cf. *Extrinsic approach*).

Introduction: see *Exposition.*

Irony (verbal irony): A figure of speech in which the actual intent is expressed in words which carry the opposite meaning.

Leitmotif/Motif: The frequent repetition of a significant phrase, image, situation or set description, which thus helps to give unity to a narrative. In stream-of-consciousness fiction, motifs serve as formal links which hold together the scattered materials of a freely associating mind.

The term *motif* is sometimes used to refer to a theme that recurs in various literary works, e.g. the "poor little rich girl" motif.

Mode of presentation: Basically there are two different ways of narrating a story. The author may tell his story in a very detailed fashion so that the reader has the feeling of participating in the action. This is called *scenic presentation*. The use of dialogue is a typical feature of scenic presentation. If the author merely gives a selective summary of what happens within a certain period we call this mode of presentation *panoramic.*

Other terms: scenic presentation = *scene* = showing
          panoramic presentation = *summary* = telling.

Narrating time: The time it takes to tell or read a story. (Cf. *Acting time, Compression* and *Expansion*).

Narrator: see *Point of view.*

Observer-narrator: see *Point of view.*

Omniscience: see *Point of view.*

Panoramic presentation: see *Mode of presentation.*
Plot: The arrangement made by the writer of the events of a story, an arrangement designed to show mainly cause and effect.
Point of view: The *author* who writes a story is always omniscient. He may choose to reveal his omniscience (unlimited knowledge), reduce it, or give it up completely. *Author* and *narrator* are not identical. The *author* is the story-teller, the "real man" with a personal biography, who remains outside the story. The *narrator* is always a figure within the story, where he can adopt various roles.
Neutral omniscience: The narrative is told in the third person. The prevailing characteristic is that the narrator knows everything about his characters, their thoughts, feelings, perceptions. The reader has access to all possible kinds of information.
Selective omniscience: The third-person narrator deliberately limits his total omniscience and restricts himself to the viewpoint of one or several *(multiple selective omniscience)* characters in the narrative. In the latter case he may shift from the viewpoint of one character to that of another *(shifting point of view)*.
Observer-narrator: The narrator confines himself to the role of an observer, who tells only those things that can be perceived from the outside. He has no access to the thoughts and feelings of other characters.
"I" as witness: The author hands his job of story-telling completely over to another mediator. The "I" as witness is a character in his own right within the story. The natural consequence of this narrative form is that the witness has no more than ordinary access to the mental state of others.
"I" as protagonist: The main character tells his own story in the first person. He is limited almost entirely to his own thoughts, feelings and perceptions.
"Withdrawal of author and narrator": The total elimination of the narrator. The story comes directly through the minds of the characters. The aim is to dramatize mental states. See *Stream of consciousness.*
The dramatic mode: Having eliminated the author, and then the narrator, we are now ready to dispose of mental states altogether. The information available to the reader in the dramatic mode is limited largely to what the characters do and say, the "point of view" being comparable to that of a camera. The characters' appearance and the setting may be supplied by the author as in the stage directions of a play. (Cf. *Scenic presentation*).
Protagonist: The hero, the main character of a literary work of art.
Reported thought: see *Stream of consciousness.*

Rising action: see *Falling action.*
Scene, scenic presentation: see *Mode of presentation.*
Setting: The physical, and sometimes spiritual, background against which the action of a narrative takes place. The elements which go to make up a setting are: a) the actual geographical location and such physical arrangements as the location of the windows and doors in a room; b) the occupations and daily manner of living of the *characters;* c) the time or period in which the *action* takes place; d) the general environment of the characters.
Story: "A narrative of events in their time-sequence" (E. M. Forster, *Aspects of the Novel,* p. 93).
Stream of consciousness: We may define stream-of-consciousness fiction as a type of fiction in which the basic emphasis is placed on the exploration of a character's consciousness for the purpose of revealing his mental nature. The important characteristic of the movement of consciousness is its ability to move freely in time and space, imitating the psychological principle of free association, controlled by memory, senses, imagination. There are two basic techniques used in presenting stream of consciousness: reported thought and interior monologue.
Reported thought (also: *indirect interior monologue* or *substitutionary narration*): a presentation of thoughts, feelings, perceptions which contains elements of both direct speech and reported speech. Typical features are the third person point of view, the past tense group (as in reported speech) and the omission of introductory clauses such as "he said", "she thought", etc.
Interior monologue (also: *direct interior monologue*): the type of monologue which presents consciousness directly to the reader. There is complete or near-complete disappearance of the author from the page. It is in the first person, the tense is as the mind dictates.
Structure: The arrangement of the material of a narrative which gives it unity and form.
Substitutionary narration: see *Stream of consciousness.*
Summary: see *Mode of presentation.*
Suspense: see *Tension.*
Symbol: An object, character, or event that represents something which is more important than the literal meaning or concrete reference.
Tension, Suspense: In a "tense situation" a particular state of affairs might at any moment be transformed into something crucially different. Hence the reader feels intense interest or excitement at such phases, he is kept in *suspense,* i.e. he is uncertain about the outcome of an action and the way it

is to be brought about. Tension is inherent in the narrative, whereas suspense refers to the relationship between the reader and the narrative.
Theme: The central or dominating idea in a literary work. In non-fiction prose it is the general topic of discussion, the subject of the discourse.
Turning-point: The point at which the action takes another direction. (Cf. *Crisis*).